RALF DAHRENDORF ON CLASS & SOCIETY

I0127679

Volume 3

HOMO SOCIOLOGICUS

HOMO SOCIOLOGICUS

RALF DAHRENDORF

Routledge
Taylor & Francis Group

LONDON AND NEW YORK

First published in Great Britain in 1968 and reprinted, with a new preface and minor revisions in 1973 by Routledge & Kegan Paul Ltd.

This edition first published in 2022
by Routledge
2 Park Square, Milton Park, Abingdon, Oxon OX14 4RN

and by Routledge
605 Third Avenue, New York, NY 10158

Routledge is an imprint of the Taylor & Francis Group, an informa business

British Library Cataloguing in Publication Data
A catalogue record for this book is available from the British Library

ISBN: 978-1-03-219648-0 (Set)
ISBN: 978-1-00-326063-9 (Set) (ebk)
ISBN: 978-1-03-219676-3 (Volume 3) (hbk)
ISBN: 978-1-03-219727-2 (Volume 3) (pbk)
ISBN: 978-1-00-326057-8 (Volume 3) (ebk)

DOI: 10.4324/9781003260578

Publisher's Note
The publisher has gone to great lengths to ensure the quality of this reprint but points out that some imperfections in the original copies may be apparent.

Disclaimer
The publisher has made every effort to trace copyright holders and would welcome correspondence from those they have been unable to trace.

Homo Sociologicus

RALF DAHRENDORF

London   Routledge & Kegan Paul

First published in German, these essays have been translated by the author. For the history of the essays see pp. 91–4.

First published in Great Britain in 1968 in Ralf Dahrendorf, 'Essays in the Theory of Society', *and reprinted, with a new preface and minor revisions, in 1973 by Routledge & Kegan Paul, Ltd Broadway House, 68–74 Carter Lane, London EC4V 5EL*

Printed in Great Britain
By Unwin Brothers Limited
The Gresham Press, Old Woking, Surrey, England
A member of the Staples Printing Group

ISBN 0 7100 7710 6 (c)
ISBN 0 7100 7711 4 (p)

Preface

When I wrote this little book in 1957 in the intelligent company and leisurely environment provided by the Center for Advanced Study in the Behavioral Sciences (and at the comparatively youthful age of 28), I certainly did not anticipate that it would still find a public more than fifteen years later. Even at the time, the essay was regarded by some as an early summary of British and American theories of roles for the edification of German students eager to catch up with international developments. However, while this may have been one of the effects of the study—another one of similarly restricted significance being that for the author it was an exercise of learning by writing—there are obviously aspects of this piece which have a more enduring quality, and which therefore warrant its republication.

One of these lasting aspects of *Homo Sociologicus* is the simple one that it is an attempt to structure an elementary and possibly universal experience from which all social science begins. Man's behaviour in this world of men is not random. It follows certain rules which, while they are like everything human, historical and thus subject to change, acquire a life of their own. Human behaviour in a given context is predictable to the extent of making the individual actors interchangeable. The official behind the counter and the citizen before it are in a sense not unique personalities, but *personae*, masks, they are playing parts, roles. All the world's a stage, or—more precisely, if less graciously put—the crystallization of rules into roles is the basic fact of society and thus of social science.

The latter however does not necessarily follow from the former; basic experiences do not have to be basic instruments of analysis. The

suggestion that in the case of roles this transformation would nevertheless be useful, may be the second durable feature in this essay. I have
not elaborated this notion at all sufficiently in the short presentation
of *Homo Sociologicus*. In fact, role theory seems to me to the present
day a largely unexploited resource of sociological analysis. This is
true above all if its force is sought less in the interpretation of man's
struggles with society, as in the masterly writings of Erving Goffman,
than in the more abstract endeavour of a *Theory of Social Structure* (to
quote the title of a series of lectures by S. F. Nadel which should not
be forgotten). Genesis and change of norms, effect of sanctions, the
division of labour and other general problems are capable of analysis
in terms of a sophisticated role approach which adds to their clarification, helps in the formulation of theoretically relevant research
designs, and lends itself to the analysis of complex specific problems
notably in the natural history of total societies. There are but hints
at these possibilities in this essay, but I continue to hope that they will
inspire the sociological imagination of others as they have stimulated
mine (though the semi-finished study of *Elements of Sociology* which
I began along these lines several years ago has now fallen victim to
those other roles which have been allocated to me).

It is difficult to ignore the fact that the description of possibly durable
aspects of this essay involves in itself a problem of considerable depth:
What does it mean that in our experience and, almost as a matter of
principle, in sociological analysis we are capable of separating visible
human actors from the moulds which shape their actions, the patterns
to which they conform, or which they confirm by not conforming to
them? This is, prima facie, a problem of philosophical anthropology;
and in fact much anthropological reflection has arisen from the experience that all the world may be a stage, and that human beings in the
world may be actors in the dual sense of the word. I have always
preferred to pose such philosophical problems with what Brecht
called a *v-effect*, an effect of deliberate estrangement (*Verfremdung*), as
problems of the logic of scientific discovery, or indeed the ethic of
scientific discovery: what are we doing if we develop theories which
imply an image of man as a composite of roles? Are there any reasons
to justify the pragmatic implications of this method?

Such questions are not limited to any particular time; in that sense
they point to another durable quality of *Homo Sociologicus*. I am,
however, more concerned about the fact that the way in which I have

posed these questions in 1957, and in which I may have indicated a possible solution, is liable to be cheerfully misinterpreted by the new romantics of the 1970s. In talking about the "vexatious fact of society", and of the individual threatened by an "artificial" world of roles, I did not mean to imply that the only, or indeed any solution might be found in an attempt to "leave" society, or to "re-constitute" an individual without roles. This raises, to be sure, complicated questions which have been impressively put by Marx in his "Economic and Philosophic Manuscripts" of 1844. Suffice it to say here that for me, the world is a stage to the extent that man without roles is man "sans teeth, sans eyes, sans taste, sans everything". Liberty therefore is, and is by necessity, liberty in society, a free society, and not liberty apart from society, freedom from society.

The possibility of this misunderstanding indicates one imperfection of this essay. It is but one of many, and not the worst, especially since I have addressed myself to that particular problem in the critical discussion of "Sociology and Human Nature" which, since it was written in 1963, has been added to all editions of *Homo Sociologicus*, and which is therefore included in this volume too. The literature quoted in this book is by now at best classical, and at worst out-dated, but in any case old; much has been published since which would force me to modify or elaborate positions. But somehow, the more time elapses, the more difficult does it become to envisage such a cosmetic operation on something that has become characteristic in its own ways for many. The reader may infer from this Preface that after all these years the author of *Homo Sociologicus* still sees no reason to denounce his creature beyond the critical reserve implicit in the analysis itself.

R.D.

Muffendorf, February 1973

Contents

1

Homo Sociologicus
On the History, Significance, and Limits of the Category of Social Role

Ordinarily, we do not much care that the table, the roast, and the wine of the scientist are paradoxically different from the table, the roast, and the wine of our everyday experience. If we want to put down a glass or write a letter, a table seems a suitable support. It is smooth, solid, and even, and a physicist would scarcely disturb us by observing that the table is "in reality" a most unsolid beehive of nuclear particles. Nor can the chemist spoil our enjoyment of the dinner by dissolving roast and wine into elements that we could hardly be tempted to consume as such. As long as we do not approach the paradox of the scientific table and the everyday table with philosophic intent, we solve it in a simple manner. We act as if the table of the physicist and our own table are two different things that have no relevant relation to each other. While we are quite prepared to concede to the physicist that his table is a most important and useful object for him, we are at the same time satisfied with our table precisely because it is not a multiply perforated beehive of moving particles.[1]

The dilemma is less easily solved when we turn to the biological sciences, especially to the biology of man. There is something unsettling about viewing a glass model of a man in an exhibition, or

[1] In an unpublished paper on "Paradox and Discovery," the Cambridge philosopher John Wisdom has discussed the paradox of the two tables at some length. For Wisdom, this paradox and others of its kind are the starting points of a well-considered metaphysics that inquires into the epistemological basis of statements without regard to their logical structure and empirical validity.

standing before an X-ray machine oneself and being "made trans-parent," or indeed carrying about the X-ray picture of one's own insides in a large envelope. Does the doctor see something inside me that I don't know about? Is this photograph me? The closer we come to ourselves, to man, the more disquieting becomes the difference between the object of naïve experience and its scientific reconstruc-tion. It is clearly no accident that whereas the terms of physics play little part in our everyday language and those of chemistry little more except as they relate to the analysis of foodstuffs, many biologi-cal categories have become a part of our direct experience of the world; that whereas protons and electrons, electromagnetic fields and the speed of light, are still alien to everyday language and we only occasionally speak of "acids," "fats," "carbohydrates," and "al-bumins," we speak all the time of "organs" and their "functions," of "nerves," "muscles," "veins," and even "brain cells."

But whatever the biologist may reveal to us about ourselves, we still have the quasi-consolation that our body is not the "real" us, that biological concepts and theories cannot affect the integrity of our individuality. We must assimilate biological man to some ex-tent, but it costs us relatively little to identify with him. I am not aware that biological categories have ever been invoked to dispute the physical uniqueness of each person. Nobody seems to feel that he has to defend his moustache, the shape of his nose, or the length of his arms against scientific references to hair growth, the nasal bones, or the humerus in order not to be robbed of his individuality and reduced to a mere illustration of general categories or principles. A charge of this kind is heard only when science extends the borders of its artificial world to take in man as an acting, thinking, feeling creature—when it becomes social science.

Social science has so far presented us with at least two new and highly problematical creatures whom we are unlikely ever to en-counter in our everyday experience. One is the much-debated *homo oeconomicus* of modern economics: the consumer who carefully weighs utility and cost before every purchase and compares hun-dreds of prices before he makes his decision; the entrepreneur who has the latest information from all markets and stock exchanges and bases his every decision on this information; the perfectly informed, thoroughly rational man. In our everyday experience this is a strange creature, and yet the concept has proved almost as useful for the economist as the beehive-table for the physicist. By and large, the facts of economic life confirm the economist's theories, and while his assumptions may appear strange and incredible, they enable him to make accurate predictions. And yet, can we still identify light-heartedly with *homo oeconomicus?* Can we, on the other hand, afford to ignore him as we do the table of the physicist?

The paradox of our relation to a second "man" of social science, psychological man (as Philip Rieff called him), is more threatening still. The godfather of psychological man was Sigmund Freud, and with Freud this new creature soon acquired considerable prominence both inside and outside scientific psychology. Psychological man is the man who even if he always does good may always want to do evil—the man of invisible motives who has not become the more familiar for our having made him into a kind of party game. You hate me? That merely means that "in reality" you love me. Nowhere is the impossibility of separating the scientific from the everyday object as overwhelming as in the case of psychological man; nowhere, therefore, is it more obviously necessary, if not to reconcile the two worlds, at least to make their separate existence comprehensible and thus bearable.

In general, economists and psychologists have not been prepared to face the contradiction between their artificial human being and the real one; their critics have usually belonged only marginally to the profession. Perhaps their attitude is right, for we have apparently grown so accustomed to *homo oeconomicus* and psychological man that a protest against these concepts is rarely heard. But our acceptance of the "men" of economics and psychology does not make the dilemma they stand for any less real. Moreover, with the rapid development of social science two new scientific "men" are coming into being: the men of sociology and political science. At a time when the discussion about their elder brothers has hardly died down, it is being revived to cast doubt on the right to existence of *homo sociologicus* and *homo politicus,* or even to prevent their birth at the last moment. Just as a shadow follows the person who casts it, so the protest against the incompatibility of the worlds of common sense and of science (always alive behind the appearance of calm) follows the paths of human inquiry.

Perhaps it is appropriate today to cease our vain and debilitating effort to run away from the shadow, and to turn and face the threat. How does the human being of our everyday experience relate to the glass men of social science? Must we and can we defend our artificial, abstract creatures against real human beings? Are we facing here a paradox analogous to that of the two tables, or is the dilemma of the social scientist's abstraction something different?

Noble and impressive though the definition of sociology as the "science of man" may be, such vague phrases tell us little about the specific subject matter of the discipline. Even the unreconstructed optimist will not claim that sociology enables him to solve the riddle of man for good. Sociology certainly is a science of man, but it is not the only such science, nor can it reasonably aspire to tackle the problem of man in all its depth and breadth. Man in his entirety not only is safely removed from the attack of any single discipline, but may possibly remain forever a nebulous shape in the background of scientific endeavor. Every discipline, if it is to make its statements precise and testable, must reduce its huge subject matter to certain elements from which may be systematically constructed, if not a portrait of the reality of experience, then a structure in whose tissue a segment of reality may be caught.

The problems of sociology all refer us to one fact that is as accessible to our experience as the natural facts of our environment. This is the fact of society, of which we are reminded so often and so intensely that there are good reasons to call it the vexatious fact of society. Mere random probability can hardly explain our behavior toward others and toward ourselves. We obey laws, go to the polls, marry, attend schools and universities, have an occupation, and are members of a church; we look after our children, lift our hats to our superiors, defer to our elders, speak to different people in different tongues, feel that we belong here and are strangers there. We cannot walk a step or speak a sentence without there intervening between us and the world a third element, one that ties us to the world and at the same time mediates between these two concrete abstractions: society.

If there is any explanation for the late birth of a science of society, we may look for it in the omnipresence of the subject matter of that science, which includes even its own description and analysis. Sociology is concerned with man in the face of the vexatious fact of society. Man, every man, encounters this fact, indeed *is* this fact; for society, while it may be conceived independently of particular individuals, would nevertheless be a meaningless fiction without particular individuals.[2] Therefore, for the elements of a science that has as its subject matter man in society, we have to look in the area where man and the fact of society intersect.

There have been many attempts in the history of sociology to find such elements. More than twenty years ago, Talcott Parsons (following Florian Znaniecki) enumerated and discussed four such approaches (30: 30). None of the four, however, satisfies the demands of sociological analysis. It sounds trivial to require that the elements of sociological analysis be sought in the area where the individual and society intersect. Nevertheless, two of Parsons's four approaches did not satisfy this requirement. Among American sociologists especially, it was popular early in our century to seek the unit of sociological analysis in the social group. Society—so Charles Cooley argued, for example—is not composed of individuals, but of groups; the sociologist is not concerned with Mr. Smith, but with the Smith family, with company X, party Y, and church Z. Now it is clearly true that the individual encounters society in social groups; this happens in a very real sense indeed. But possibly this encounter is too real. In the group the individual disappears; if the group is

[2] The relation between what I have called here the "vexatious fact of society" and Durkheim's "social facts," facts that force us into their spell, is evident. In the beginning of the first chapter of his *Règles* of 1895, Durkheim described "social facts" as follows: "If I fulfill my obligations as brother, husband, or citizen, if I honor my contracts, I perform duties that are defined without reference to myself and my actions in law and custom. Even if these duties are in accord with my own sentiments and I feel subjectively their reality, such reality is objective, for I have not created it; I have merely inherited it as a result of my education." In this passage Durkheim comes close to the category of role discussed in this essay.

taken as the element of analysis, there is no way left for the sociologist to find the individual as a social animal. If, on the other hand
—as often happens to this day—we take as our elementary unit the
personality, even the social personality, of the individual, it becomes difficult to account for the fact of society. Speaking of groups
means removing the focus of analysis entirely to grounds outside the
individual; speaking of social personalities involves complete con-
centration on the individual himself. The problem is to find an elementary category in which both the individual and society can be
accommodated.

Most modern sociologists have thought they could satisfy the need
for an elementary analytical category by using as their basis either
(with Leopold von Wiese) the concept of "social relations," or (with
Max Weber) that of "social action." It is not difficult to see, however,
that both of these concepts leave our problem unsolved. Speaking
of "social relations" or "social action" is hardly less general than
speaking of "man" or "society." We still do not know the elements
of which "social relations" and "social action" are composed, the
categories, that is, with which to describe the relations between men
in society or the socially determined action of men.

It is no accident, therefore, that the contemporary proponents of
"social relations" and "social action" introduce in the course of
their analyses, or even in their conceptual considerations, further
categories that come nearer to being the elementary analytical units
that sociology needs. Von Wiese and Parsons refer in related ways
on the one hand to "social formations" or "social systems" as structural units of society, and on the other to "offices" or "roles" as the
individual's crystallized modes of participation in the social process.
Neither pair of categories can in any way be derived from the general concepts "social relations" and "social action"; one is tempted
to suggest that their authors have introduced them almost against
their will. And while this may be rather less than conclusive proof
of sociology's need for such categories, it is at least plausible evidence; and it seems worth reflecting on why the authors found it
necessary to introduce them.

At the point where individual and society intersect stands *homo* *sociologicus*, man as the bearer of socially predetermined roles. To a sociologist the individual *is* his social roles, but these roles, for their part, are the vexatious fact of society. In solving its problems, sociology necessarily takes social roles as its elements of analysis; its subject matter is the structure of social roles. But by reconstructing man as *homo sociologicus* in this manner, sociology creates for itself once again the moral and philosophical problem of how the artificial man of its theoretical analysis relates to the real man of our everyday experience. If sociology is not to fall victim to an uncritical scientism, the attempt to sketch in some dimensions of the category of social role must not lose sight of the moral problem created by the artificiality of its model. If, on the other hand, philosophical criticism is to go beyond irrelevant generalities, it presupposes a thorough understanding of the uses and abuses of the category of social role.[*]

II

The attempt to reduce man to *homo sociologicus* for the sake of solving certain problems is neither as arbitrary nor as recent as one might think. Like *homo oeconomicus* and psychological man, man as the bearer of social roles is not primarily a description of reality, but a scientific construct. Yet however much scientific activity may resemble a game, it would be wrong to regard it as irrelevant to the reality of experience. The paradoxes of the physicist's table and the everyday table, the sociologist's man and the man on the street, are by no means the end and aim of science; rather they are an entirely unsought and troublesome consequence of the scientist's effort to investigate otherwise inaccessible segments of the world. In an important sense, the atom and the social role, though inventions, are not *merely* inventions. They are categories that at many times and

---

[*] Reflection about the elements of sociological analysis is at any point reflection about sense and nonsense, about the uses and abuses of sociology as a science. However, it takes us beyond the mere exchange of pre-existing opinions. Even though we do not make the defense or critique of sociology our explicit aim, the terms of this essay should enable us to put an end once and for all to the still lingering dispute over the limits and possibilities of a science of society.

places, and under various names, have suggested themselves with an inexplicable necessity to scientists bent on understanding nature, or man in society. Once invented, they are not merely meaningful, i.e. operationally useful, but also plausible. In a certain sense, they are self-evident categories.

Remarkably enough, both the atom and the role were given their present names when the concepts were first invented, and both names have remained the same through the centuries. With respect to the atom, the explanation is evident; the word ἄτομον speaks for itself,[4] and the concept as now used refers consciously to its first use by Democritus. The development of the concept of social role is more complicated and more instructive. It can be shown that in trying to describe the point of contact between the individual and society many writers—poets, scholars, philosophers—have introduced identical or at least related concepts. The words we encounter time and again in this context are *mask, persona, character,* and *role* or *part.* Although there is a conscious terminological tradition here as with the atom, it would seem that many writers have independently come up not merely with the same concept, but with the same name for the concept—as if to prove that names have some content after all.

Role, part, persona, character, and *mask* are words whose basic context, allowing for different stages of the development of language, is the same, namely the theater. We speak of the *dramatis personae* or characters of the play, whose part or role the actor plays; and if nowadays he does not usually wear a mask, the word is no less clearly of theatrical origin. These words have a number of characteristics in common. (1) All of them indicate something that is given to an actor for the occasion, something that is outside himself. (2) This "something" may be described as a complex of modes of behavior, which (3) in turn connects with other such complexes to form a whole, and is in that sense a "part" (as the Latin *pars* and the English "part" for the actor's role still indicate). (4) Since these

[4] This example shows, however, that the literal meaning of words must not be overestimated as a clue to their present connotations. In terms of literal meaning, "atom" and "individual" cannot be differentiated; nor does the literal meaning of "individual" tell us that the individual is the basic unit of social science.

modes of behavior are given to the actor, he must learn them in order to be able to play his part. (5) From the point of view of the actor, no role, no *dramatis persona*, is exhaustive; he can learn and play a multitude of roles.

In addition to these five characteristics of theatrical roles, there is a further consideration that takes us to the limits of the stage metaphor. This is that behind all roles, personas, and masks the actor remains a real being, a person in no way affected by the parts he plays.[5] His stage roles are for him superficial, something apart from his inner being. He is "himself" only when he casts them off—or, as John of Salisbury says in his *Policraticus* of 1159 (see 7: 146): "The troupe presents a farce on the stage; one man is called 'Father,' another 'Son,' and the third 'Rich Man.' Soon, when the script-book is shut on these comic roles, the true face returns, the mask vanishes." John of Salisbury's lines are no longer a description of the theater. Indeed, the stage metaphor—as E. R. Curtius has shown by various examples—is a very old device of philosophy and poetry. Among its early uses Curtius mentions Plato's *Laws*, with its notion of living creatures as puppets of divine origin, and his *Philebus*, with its image of the "tragedy and comedy of life" (33: I, 644d–e, 34: 50b). Seneca uses the same image when he refers to "this drama of human life, wherein we are assigned the parts that we are to play so badly" (40: 80, 7). From St. Paul to John of Salisbury and right up to the present day, the metaphor is frequently found in Christian writings.[6] In time the notion of the *theatrum mundi* becomes almost commonplace. It is used by Luther and Shakespeare, by Calderón and Cervantes. Hofmannsthal's *Great Salzburg World Theater* is but one recent proof that the device is still with us.

Strictly speaking, however, the *theatrum mundi* metaphor is only indirect evidence for the substantive necessity and age-old use of the category of role in the sense of this essay. For insofar as the world is seen as a gigantic play, each player is given just one mask, one persona, one character, one role in it all (by a divine "director,"

[5] This statement is meant in an essential sense. Obviously, an actor may sometimes find it hard, on leaving the stage, to cast off a part that—as we say—he has "lived."
[6] One need but think of the understanding of the trinity as a unity of three "persons," notably in the work of Augustinus.

who has been part of the metaphor since Plato's time). But it was our intention to go beyond this one-dimensional view of man. Our aim is to dissolve human action into its components, and by analyzing these components to arrive at a rational understanding of the whole. In the circumstances, we do well to turn from the *theatrum mundi* to a more manageable use of the theatrical metaphor: its application to the life of the individual, in the sense of attributing to a given person several roles or personas.

This is an old notion, too. It probably found its earliest expression in terms of the Latin word *persona,* or the corresponding Greek word, πρόσωπον. Cicero gives us a nice illustration for the use of *persona* in this sense:

> We must realize also that we are invested by Nature with two characters [*personis*], as it were. One of these is universal, arising from the fact of our being all alike endowed with reason and with that superiority which lifts us above the brute. From this all morality and propriety are derived, and upon it depends the rational method of ascertaining our duty. The other character is the one that is assigned to individuals in particular. (6: I, 107.)

These two natural roles, the result of a general human endowment and a specific individual endowment, have little in common with social roles; but Cicero goes on to say:

> To the two above-mentioned characters [*personis*] is added a third, which some chance or some circumstance imposes, and a fourth also, which we assume by our own deliberate choice. Regal powers and military commands, nobility of birth and political office, wealth and influence, and their opposites depend upon chance and are, therefore, controlled by circumstances. But what role we ourselves may choose to sustain is decided by our own free choice. And so some turn to philosophy, others to the civil law, and still others to oratory, while in the case of the virtues themselves one man prefers to excel in one, another in another. (6: I, 115.)

Cicero's reflections presumably echo a lost work of Panaetius (περὶ τοῦ καθήκοντος), for whom the individual personality was similarly composed of four personas, each to some extent inborn and individual but also to some extent acquired and social. Both Panaetius and Cicero define all four personas as largely inborn or inherent, although the last two may have external causes and limits. From something given to the individual, something outside him, *persona* in Cicero's use has already become a part of the individual; and the same semantic process has consistently led later writers to use "persona" to epitomize the individuality of man. The word "character" (χαρακτήρ: that which is stamped, the impression) has had much the same fate. Similarly, as we shall see, "role," which once meant a predetermined behavior pattern, has increasingly been used by social scientists to refer to an individual's customary or habitual behavior, being thus transformed from a category of sociology into a category of social psychology. Badly as we need a category like "role," "persona," or "character" to describe what happens at the point where the individual and society intersect, it seems difficult to restrict such words to this function.

Not all writers, however, have found it hard to focus on role in our sense of the word. In *As You Like It* Shakespeare puts into Jaques's mouth a speech that eminently anticipates the nature and potential of the category of social role, and thus illuminates many features of the sociological concept of role (II. vii):

All the world's a stage,
And all the men and women merely players:
They have their exits and their entrances;
And one man in his time plays many parts,
His acts being seven ages. At first the infant,
Mewling and puking in the nurse's arms.
Then the whining schoolboy, with his satchel
And shining morning face, creeping like snail
Unwillingly to school. And then the lover,
Sighing like furnace, with a woeful ballad
Made to his mistress' eyebrow. Then a soldier,
Full of strange oaths, and bearded like the pard,
Jealous in honor, sudden and quick in quarrel,
Seeking the bubble reputation

Even in the cannon's mouth. And then the justice,
In fair round belly with good capon lin'd,
With eyes severe and beard of formal cut,
Full of wise saws and modern instances;
And so he plays his part. The sixth age shifts
Into the lean and slipper'd pantaloon,
With spectacles on nose and pouch on side,
His youthful hose, well sav'd, a world too wide
For his shrunk shank; and his big manly voice,
Turning again toward childish treble, pipes
And whistles in his sound. Last scene of all,
That ends this strange eventful history,
Is second childishness and mere oblivion,
Sans teeth, sans eyes, sans taste, sans everything.

Shakespeare's main concern here is with age roles, which are only one class of social roles, but the speech at least hints at occupational and other roles. "The world" is a stage, which players enter and leave. But each player makes more than one appearance, and every one in a different mask. The same player enters the stage as a child and leaves it to return as a young man, a grown man, and an old man. Only when he dies does he have his last exit; but by then new and different players are on the stage playing "his" parts.

Today, Shakespeare's metaphor has become the central principle of the science of society. From the sociological point of view, the idea that relates the individual meaningfully to society is the idea of the individual as a bearer of socially predetermined attributes and modes of behavior. Jack Smith as a schoolboy, with a satchel and a shining morning face, creeps unwillingly to school; as a lover, he sighs and sings a ballad to his beloved; as a soldier, he wears a beard, curses, is quarrelsome and jealous of his honor; as a judge, he dresses carefully and is full of wise saws. "Schoolboy," "lover," "soldier," "judge," and "old man" are in a strange way both this particular individual, Jack Smith, and something that can be separated from him and spoken of without reference to him. Shakespeare's judge may no longer be appropriate for the stage of our time, but we too can say what a judge is like, whether his name is Jack Smith or John O'Connor. In our time as in Shakespeare's, it is the vexatious fact of society that wrests the individual out of his individuality and defines his being by the alien categories of the world outside himself.

The fact of society is vexatious because we cannot escape it. There may be lovers who neither sigh nor make a woeful ballad to their mistress's eyebrow, but such lovers do not play their role; in the language of modern American sociology, they are deviants. For every position a person can occupy—whether it is described in terms of age, family, occupation, nationality, class membership, or what have you—"society" has defined certain personal qualities and modes of behavior as acceptable. The incumbent of such a position must decide whether or not to behave as society says he must. If he yields to society's demands, he abandons his virgin individuality but gains society's approval. If he resists society's demands, he may preserve an abstract and bootless independence, but only at the expense of incurring society's wrath and painful sanctions. It is with this decision that *homo sociologicus* is born, along with man as a social being. With this decision begins that "appearance as" on the stage of life which Cicero tries to catch in the concept of *persona*, Marx in the concept of "character mask,"[7] and Shakespeare, along with most modern sociologists, in the concept of "part" or "role."

It is understandable that the idea of social role has repeatedly been described in theatrical terms. What could be more plausible than an analogy between prescribed behavior patterns for actors in given parts and socially defined behavior norms for persons in given positions? And yet such an analogy may be misleading. Whereas the unreality of events is assumed in the theater, it cannot be assumed with respect to society. Despite the theatrical connotations of "role," it would be wrong to see the role-playing social personality as an unreal person who has merely to drop his mask to appear

---

[7] Marx refers at several points to the "character mask" of the capitalist or the bourgeois. In a similar sense he distinguishes at one point (22: 8) between (1) the "persons of the capitalist and the landowner" and (2) capitalist and landowner as "personifications of economic categories," i.e. as social roles. For examples of the use of "character mask" and other concepts, see section VII below.

as his true self. *Homo sociologicus* and the undivided individual
of our experience stand in a dangerous and paradoxical relationship, one that it would be wrong to ignore or minimize. The charac-
terization of man as a social being is more than a metaphor. His
roles are more than masks that can be cast off, his social behavior
more than a play from which audience and actors alike can return
to the "true" reality.

III

Perhaps it is a little unfair to stress the vexation of *homo sociologicus,* inevitable though it is, before this new man has had the
chance to prove himself. We have introduced the forefathers of
sociological man, we have discussed the problems with which he
confronts us, but so far we have not asked precisely who he is and
what his capacities are. To be sure, we could simply point out that
homo sociologicus figures prominently in the works of contemporary social scientists, and suggest that these works be consulted for
a summary of his properties. Such a course, however, would lead
us into difficulties. For agreed though many sociologists are on the
name of their creature, they have very different ideas of his nature.
Let us therefore ignore the contradictory literature on our subject,
and address ourselves to it directly. We shall begin with the context
of observation and theory in which *homo sociologicus* emerges, and
only afterward measure our findings against those of other sociologists.[8]

Let us assume that at a party we are introduced to a Herr Doktor
Hans Schmidt.[9] We are curious to find out more about our new
acquaintance. Who is Hans Schmidt? Some of the answers to this
question we can see right away. Hans Schmidt is (1) a man; more

[8] The following analysis is nonetheless oriented throughout to the sociological
discussion of the categories in question. We are forgoing an explicit critical discussion
at this point in the hope of taking in stride certain hurdles that the conceptual debate
has so far been unable to get past. Where the following discussion is directly de-
pendent on the work of others, the usual acknowledgments are made.

[9] It would have been easy to give Herr Schmidt an English name, but not so easy
to translate all his roles, every one of which has clear cultural connotations. Since it
is useful for the subsequent argument if these cultural connotations stand out clearly,
I have left Herr Schmidt his original German name.

precisely, (2) an adult man about 35 years of age. He is wearing a wedding ring, and is therefore (3) married. The context of his introduction tells us further that Hans Schmidt is (4) a citizen, (5) a German, (6) an inhabitant of town X, and, since he has the title of Doktor, (7) a professional man. Everything else we have to find out from mutual acquaintances. They may tell us that Herr Schmidt is (8) a grammar school teacher by profession, (9) the father of two children, (10) a Protestant in the predominantly Catholic population of X, and (11) a former refugee who came to X after the war; that he has made a good name for himself by becoming (12) vice-chairman of the local organization of the Y party and (13) treasurer of the local soccer club; and finally that he is (14) a passionate and excellent card player, and (15) an equally passionate, though less excellent, driver. His friends, colleagues, and acquaintances have much more to tell us about Herr Schmidt, but with the information we have acquired, our curiosity is satisfied for the time being. Among other things, we feel that Herr Schmidt is no longer a stranger to us now. What is behind this feeling?

It might be argued that what we have found out about Herr Schmidt does not really distinguish him from other men. Not only Herr Schmidt but many other men are Germans, fathers, Protestants, and grammar school teachers; and if there is only one treasurer of the local soccer club at any given time, there were others before him, so that this office, too, is not unique to Herr Schmidt. Indeed, our information about Herr Schmidt refers without exception to certain places that he occupies, i.e., to points in a co-ordinate system of social relations. For the informed, every position implies a net of other positions connected with it, a position field. As a father, Herr Schmidt stands in one position field with his wife, his son, and his daughter; as a schoolmaster, he is related to his pupils, their parents, his colleagues, and the officials of the school administration; as vice-chairman of the Y party, he is related to his colleagues on the party committee, to higher party officials, to other party members, and to the voting public. Some of these position fields overlap, but no two are identical. Every one of the fifteen positions of Herr Schmidt that we know about has its own position field.

The term *social position* designates every place in a field of social relations, if we extend the concept of social relations to include
not merely positions like grammar school teacher and vice-chairman
of the Y party, but also father, German, and card player. Positions
may in principle be thought of independently of their incumbents.
Just as the mayor's office and the professor's chair do not cease to
exist when they become vacant, the positions of Herr Schmidt do
not depend on his personality or even his existence. A man not only
can, but as a rule must, assume a number of positions, and it may
be supposed that the number grows with the complexity of the society. Moreover, the position field corresponding to a given position may consist of a multitude of distinct referents, as with Herr
Schmidt's positions of grammar school teacher and treasurer of the
local soccer club; that is, positions may themselves be complex. It
may accordingly prove useful to see social positions as sets of *position segments,* i.e., to see the position of teacher as made up of
the position segments teacher-pupils, teacher-parents, teacher-col-
leagues, and teacher-administrators, each standing for a different
direction of relationship.

However, these conceptual distinctions and definitions cannot
explain why Herr Schmidt is no longer a stranger to us once we
know what positions he holds. For it hardly makes sense to assume
that Herr Schmidt is nothing but the aggregate of his positions, that
his individuality consists, if not in any one position, in the constel-
lation of the whole. Many of his characteristics cannot conceivably
be inferred from his positions: whether he is a good or bad teacher,
a strict or lenient father; whether or not he can control his emo-
tions; whether or not he is satisfied with his life; what he thinks
about his fellowmen when he is all by himself; where he would like
to spend his vacation.[10] Herr Schmidt is more than an incumbent of
social positions, and much that his friends know about him neither
the casual acquaintance nor the sociologist knows or wants to know.

If Herr Schmidt's positions do not tell us everything about his
personality, however, it is astonishing how much they do tell us.

[10] As these remarks suggest, in learning that Herr Schmidt is an excellent card
player but not an excellent driver, we learn more than we need to know for defining
his social positions.

The positions themselves, of course, provide us merely with the most formal sort of knowledge. They tell us what Herr Schmidt's social fields of reference are and with whom he has social relations, but they tell us nothing about the substance of these relations. And yet no further questions are needed for us to find out what this substance is: i.e., what Herr Schmidt does in his numerous positions— or in any case what he should do, and therefore probably does. As a father, Herr Schmidt looks after his children, helps them, protects them, and loves them. As a grammar school teacher, he imparts knowledge to his pupils, judges them fairly, advises their parents, shows deference to the school principal, and behaves in an exemplary fashion. As a party functionary, he attends meetings, gives speeches, and tries to sign up new members. Not only what Herr Schmidt does, but what he is like, can be derived to some extent from his positions—indeed, a man's appearance often reveals "who he is," i.e., what positions he holds. As a grammar school teacher Herr Schmidt wears a teacher's "decent" but not too expensive clothes, inclucing shiny trousers and coats with leather elbows; as a husband he wears a wedding ring; one can probably see in his demeanor whether the Y party is a radical party; his appearance is sporty; he is probably above average in intelligence and energy. This list shows that *homo sociologicus*, like psychological man, can be turned into an amusing party game with serious overtones.[11] Every position carries with it certain expected modes of behavior; every position a person occupies requires him to do certain things and exhibit certain characteristics; to every social position there belongs a *social role*. By assuming a social position, the individual becomes a character in the drama written by the society he is living in. With every position he assumes, society hands him a role to play. It is by positions and roles that two conceptually distinguishable facts, the individual and society, are mediated; and it is in terms of these two concepts that we describe *homo sociologicus*, sociological man, the basic unit of sociological analysis.

Of the two concepts, position and role, role is by far the more

11 Indeed, *homo sociologicus* has become a television game, notably on those quiz programs that feature efforts to "guess" a person's occupation from his appearance and demeanor. Without the fact of society, such programs would make no sense.

important. Positions merely identify places in fields of reference; roles tell us about how people in given positions relate to people in other positions in the same field. Social roles represent society's demands on the incumbents of social positions. These demands may be of two kinds: demands affecting behavior (*role behavior*) and demands affecting appearance and "character" (*role attributes*). Because Herr Schmidt is a grammar school teacher, certain attributes and a certain kind of behavior are required of him; the same holds for each of his other fourteen positions. Although the social role associated with a given position cannot tell us how a person in this position will actually behave, we do know, if we are familiar with the society that defines this role, what is expected of one who is assigned it. Social roles, then, are bundles of expectations directed at the incumbents of positions in a given society.

Like positions, roles are in principle conceivable without reference to particular persons. The behavior and attributes expected from the father, the grammar school teacher, the party functionary, or the card player can be described without reference to any particular father, teacher, party functionary, or card player. Finally, each of a man's social roles potentially comprises a number of *role segments*. The expectations associated with the role of grammar school teacher may be subdivided into expectations with respect to the role segments teacher-pupils, teacher-parents, and so on. Thus every role is a complex or set of behavior expectations.[12]

All too frequently, logical differences between various kinds of statements about behavior are overlooked. "Herr Schmidt went to church yesterday," "Herr Schmidt regularly goes to church on Sundays," and "Herr Schmidt as a practicing Protestant should go to church regularly on Sundays" are all statements about social be-

[12] The terms introduced in this section—"position," "position segment" ("positional sector"), "role," "role behavior," "role attributes," and "role segment" ("role sector")—may all be found in the study by Neal Gross et al. (13), chap. iv, "A Language for Role Analysis." Apart from the definition of terms, what is new in Gross's treatment is the distinction between role behavior and role attributes, and the subdivision of positions and roles into segments or sectors. Such a subdivision has been suggested also, with different terms, by Robert K. Merton in his essay "The Role-Set" (24); and the distinction between "roles" and "tasks" introduced by Talcott Parsons seems to serve a similar purpose. For more on terminological issues, see section VII below.

havior; yet they are distinguishable by more than the form of the verb. The first statement refers to something Herr Schmidt has in fact done at a specific time, a particular instance of behavior. The second sentence refers to something Herr Schmidt is doing regularly, a regular mode of behavior. The third statement refers to something Herr Schmidt should do regularly, an expected mode of behavior. Without doubt all three statements are in some sense sociologically relevant, since going to church is a form of behavior that can tell us something about a society. But only the third statement is relevant to sociological analysis; only in this statement do the individual and society appear to be related in a definite way. Both the particular behavior and the regular behavior of Herr Schmidt remain in some sense his private property. Although both help to create a social reality, and although both may serve, in surveys for example, as data for impressive tabulations, the fact of society does not appear in them as an independent and active force.

In speaking of social roles, then, we invariably refer to expected behavior; our concern is invariably with the individual as confronted with demands generated outside himself, or with society as it confronts the individual with such demands. The mediation of the individual and society is not accomplished by action in itself, or even by the establishing of social relations; it is accomplished only in the individual's active encounter with socially prescribed patterns of action. The first concern of sociology, therefore, is always with these patterns or roles; the further question of how particular individuals actually come to terms with role expectations makes sense only if we know what to make of these expectations.

Three features characterize the category of social role as an element of sociological analysis. (1) Like positions, social roles are quasi-objective complexes of prescriptions for behavior which are in principle independent of the individual. (2) Their particular content is defined and redefined not by any individual, but by society. (3) The behavior expectations associated with roles are binding on the individual, in the sense that he cannot ignore or reject them without harm to himself. These three features give rise to three recurrent questions of role theory, which we must try to answer if we are to present the case of *homo sociologicus* with any degree of precision. (1) How in detail does the encounter of individual and society occur? How do predetermined roles become a part of people's social behavior? What is the relation between *homo sociologicus* and psychological man? (2) Who or what is this "society" that serves as the defining agency of roles? Can the process of defining and redefining social roles be rendered so precise that such irritating personifications can be dispensed with? (3) How is the force of role expectations made binding? What mechanisms or institutions prevent the individual from simply dismissing the behavior prescriptions that he encounters as irrelevant and arbitrary?

IV

Clearly, it makes sense to speak of a mediation of the individual and society only where the two do not merely exist side by side, but are connected in definite ways. The statement that there is a grammar school teacher named Hans Schmidt, and that thus-and-such modes of behavior and attributes are associated with the social role of grammar school teacher, is without analytical value unless it can be shown that Herr Schmidt's relationship to his social role is neither purely accidental nor alterable by his own free decision, but a matter of necessity and constraint. It must therefore be shown that society is not merely a fact but a vexatious fact, one that we cannot ignore or flout without punishment. Social roles are a constraining force on the individual, whether he experiences them as an obstacle to his private wishes or a support that gives him security. The constraining force of role expectations is due to the availability of *sanctions*, measures by which society can enforce conformity with its prescriptions. The man who does not play his role is punished; the man who plays his role is rewarded, or at least not punished. Social pressure to conform to prescribed role expectations is by no means peculiar to certain modern societies, but a universal feature of all social forms.[13]

---

[13] Certain American "nonconformists" mistakenly believe that "keeping up with the Joneses" is an American invention. The undeniable variations from one society to another in the degree of open and hidden constraint brought to bear on their

The concept of sanction is often applied exclusively to punishments and reproofs; however, in keeping with sociological usage
we shall apply it here in a wider sense. There are positive as well
as negative sanctions: society may bestow decorations as well as
impose prison sentences, acknowledge prestige as well as expose
unacceptable behavior. Still, it seems best in the present context
to think chiefly in terms of negative sanctions. Not only is it often
difficult to characterize positive sanctions in precise and operational
terms,[14] but they do little to explain the pressure to which *homo
sociologicus* is steadily exposed. One can renounce rewards and de-
cline decorations, but to escape the force of the law or even of social disapproval is difficult in all societies. It is not only kings that
go to Canossa. Like role expectations themselves, the sanctions attached to them are subject to change; but also like role expectations, they are ubiquitous and inescapable.

The effect of sanctions is most immediately clear in the case of
role expectations supported by the force of law and legal institutions. Most social roles include such elements, certain *must-expectations*[15] that can be ignored or flouted only at the risk of legal pros-
ecution. As a man, Herr Schmidt must not have sexual relations
with other men; as a husband, he must not have extramarital sexual relations. As a grammar school teacher, he is expected to edu-
cate at least his older pupils without using the cane. If, as treasurer
of the local soccer club, he uses the club's money to pay his card-
playing debts, he incurs the negative sanctions laid down by law.
So far as the law applies to people as incumbents of positions, as to
a large extent it does, it may be understood as an aggregate of sanc-

----

individual members cannot be expressed in terms of conformism. Rather, they refer
to the range of choice left to the individual by a given society's social role definitions.
Such definitions in themselves imply a pressure to conform on all points covered.

14 This is a difficult problem, with which theorists of stratification in particular
have been struggling. One can of course develop scales of rewards such as income and
prestige, but so far the necessary connection between such rewards and role expectations has not been conclusively demonstrated. In the absence of such a connection,
there is no way of classifying role expectations by the positive sanctions associated
with them.

15 The term is chosen by analogy to the German legal term "must-prescriptions."
This holds correspondingly for the terms "shall-expectations" and "can-expectations"
introduced below.

tions by which society guarantees conformity with its role expectations. Must-expectations are the hard core of any social role. Not
only is it possible to formulate them, but they are in fact formu-
lated, or codified; and their compulsory character is nearly absolute. It may further be observed that the sanctions associated with
them are almost exclusively negative. Perhaps Herr Schmidt may
someday be awarded a plaque for "25 years' driving without an accident"; otherwise compliance with the law yields no positive profit.

But laws and law courts are by no means the only manifestations
of role expectations and sanctions. To be sure, it can be argued that
the range of legally regulated behavior increases with social development;[16] in any case this range is much larger in contemporary
developed societies than in historical or underdeveloped societies.
Nevertheless, even in present-day Germany, France, England, and
America there is a wide range of social behavior which is beyond
the reach of courts and laws (except in a metaphorical sense), and
which most citizens consider more important than the range subject to legal sanctions. If Herr Schmidt, as vice-chairman of the
local organization of the Y party, insists on proselytizing for the Z
party among his colleagues, they are unlikely to accord him much
approval even though no court of law could try him for this offense.
More precisely, no official court of law could try him. In fact, many
organizations today have developed quasi-legal institutions of their
own to enforce conformity with their behavior prescriptions. And
surely it is hardly less painful for a man to be excommunicated by
his church, expelled by his party, dismissed by his firm, or stricken
from the register of his professional organization, than to be sen-
tenced to prison by a court of law. These are extreme sanctions, but
there are also milder penalties—from silent disapproval to reproofs,
compulsory transfers, and delays in promotion—whose effects must
not be underestimated. Apart from must-expectations, then, most
social roles include certain *shall-expectations,* which are scarcely
less compulsory than must-expectations. With shall-expectations

16 This was one of the theses of the evolutionary theorists of the turn of the century; see, for example, L. T. Hobhouse's *Morals in Evolution.* The thesis clearly
has a proven core, but the borderline between custom and law is often hard to define,
especially where common law and precedent dominate.

negative sanctions still prevail, although the man who complies
with them punctiliously can be sure of the esteem of his fellowmen. Such a man "is a model of behavior"; he always "does the
right thing," and therefore "can be relied on."

By contrast, a third group of role expectations, *can-expectations*,
carry mostly positive sanctions. If Herr Schmidt spends a great deal
of his leisure time collecting funds for his party, if as a teacher he
volunteers to conduct the school orchestra or as a father he spends
every free minute with his children, he gains esteem by doing
"more than he needs to," more than his fair share. Even can-expectations do not yet bring us to the domain of unregulated social
behavior. The man who never does more than what is absolutely
necessary must have very effective alternative sources of gratifica-
tion to remain unaffected by the disapproval of his fellowmen.
This is true above all in the occupational sphere, but also in political parties, voluntary organizations, and educational institutions,
where compliance with can-expectations is frequently a condition
of advancement. Difficult as it may be to formulate the precise substance of can-expectations and the sanctions associated with them,
they play no less a part than must- and shall-expectations in the
roles that fall to us, whether we want them or not, on the stage of
society.[17]

17 Herr Schmidt's position as treasurer of the soccer club may be used to exemplify
the classes of role expectations and their sanctions:

Kind of Expectation	Kind of Sanction		Example of Behavior
	Positive	Negative	
must-expectations	——	punishment by court of law	honest financial demeanor
shall-expectations	(popularity)	social exclusion	active partic-ipation in club meetings
can-expectations	esteem	(unpopu-larity)	voluntary collection of funds

A similar classification of role expectations by degrees of compulsoriness is introduced by Gross *et al.* (13: 58ff), using the terms "permissive" (can-), "preferential"
(shall-), and "mandatory" (must-) expectations; but the absence of a reference to legal
sanctions deprives their analysis of much of its potential strength.

In classifying and defining the sanctions that enforce conformity with social role behavior, we enter the field of the sociology of law. Between must-, shall-, and can-expectations on the one hand, and law, custom, and habit on the other, there is more than an analogy; the two sets of concepts apply to identical phenomena. Just as laws can be seen as the result of an ongoing historical process by which habits crystallize into customs, customs into laws, so social roles are subject to permanent changes in this sense. And just as laws may lose validity as their social background changes, so must-expectations may lose their force. For example, whereas it was once a must-expectation in Western society that a husband would take care of his parents and his wife's parents as well, today a man gains at most a certain additional prestige by interpreting the expectation that he will love his parents as an obligation to take care of them.[18] The subtle problem of the social foundations of the legal system cannot be considered in detail here, since not all of its aspects contribute to an understanding of the category of social role. But it is useful to keep in mind that the mediation of the individual and society by social roles links the individual, *inter alia,* to the world of law and custom. Herr Schmidt plays his roles because law and custom force him to do so; but only by playing his roles does he come to perceive law and custom as definite realities, and thus become a part of the normative structure of society. The category of role, then, is a meaningful starting point also for the sociological analysis of legal norms and institutions.

It would be hard to formulate role expectations clearly were it not for the fact of sanctions, which make it possible to classify roles by the degree to which their associated expectations are compulsory. Some of Herr Schmidt's social roles involve many and far-reaching must-expectations—notably citizen, but also husband and father. Others involve no legal sanctions whatever—notably card player, but also Protestant and German. The degree of institutionalization of social roles, i.e., the extent to which the associated ex-

---

[18] The intimate connections of law and custom, and the ways in which actual behavior influences behavior expectations, may also be illustrated by the debate in many countries over the penalties attached to homosexuality and abortion.

pectations are enforced by legal sanctions, provides us with a standard for judging how significant a given role is not only to society, but to the individual as well. If we can succeed in quantifying the weight of sanctions, we shall have a means of ordering, characterizing, and distinguishing all known roles in a given society.[19]

However, just as *homo sociologicus* does not exhaust the human personality, so no one of Herr Schmidt's roles can prescribe his entire behavior in the corresponding social position. There is a range in which the individual is free to behave as he chooses. In view of our emphasis on society's vexatiousness, it becomes especially important to define this range of freedom. Clearly, it is up to father Schmidt whether he wants to play ball or electric trains with his children, and no social agency prescribes whether teacher Schmidt will gain his pupils' attention by his wit or his intellectual competence. But these areas of free decision are small in comparison to the broad areas of constraint associated with sanctioned role expectations. Indeed, the more precise we render the category of social role, the more threatening becomes the problem of *homo sociologicus*, sociological man, whose every move expresses a role imposed on him by the impersonal agency of society. Is *homo sociologicus* a totally alienated man, given into the hands of man-made powers and yet with no chance of escaping them?

We cannot yet give a precise answer to this question, which is in some ways central to these reflections. But it is worth repeating here that social roles and the associated sanctions are not merely a vexation. To be sure, people do get worried and anxious when society forces them to do things that they would not have chosen to do on their own. But society at the same time supports people and gives them security, even people who do their best to throw off their roles whenever they possibly can. It is an entirely speculative question whether anyone would be capable of shaping his entire behavior on his own, without the assistance of society. Since complete freedom has its drawbacks, as was clear long before Jean-Paul Sartre

---

[19] A beginning effort to this end has been made in an as yet unpublished dissertation by Karl F. Schumann on the theory and techniques of measuring social sanctions (39).

wrote *La Nausée*, it is at least conceivable that a human being stripped of all roles would find it very difficult indeed to make his behavior meaningful. What is more, it seems certain that many of the gratifications we experience come from our roles themselves, which is to say from constraints not of our own making. The problem of man's freedom as a social being is a problem of the balance between role-determined behavior and autonomy, and in this respect at least the analysis of *homo sociologicus* seems to confirm the dialectical paradox of freedom and necessity.

V

The parts of the actor are specified in overt ways: they are originally written by an author, and later supervised by a director, both of whom can be identified as persons. But who defines social roles and watches over their acting out? Although many recent writers would answer "society," just as we have so far, the term is hard to justify. Society is patently not a person, and any personification of it obscures its nature and weakens what is said about it. Although society is a fact, one that can cause people to stumble like a stone or a tree stump, the author and director of the social drama cannot be identified by simply pointing to the fact of society. To be sure, society consists of individuals and is in this sense created by individuals, though Herr Schmidt's particular society is perhaps more his predecessors' work than his own. On the other hand, experience suggests that in some sense society is not only more than the sum of its individual members, but something significantly different in kind. Society is the alienated persona of the individual, *homo sociologicus,* a shadow that has escaped the man to return as his master. Even if we renounce for the moment the attempt to sound the depths of this paradoxical condition, as sociologists we must still seek some way, not only of identifying the agency responsible for social rules, but of describing this agency with operational precision. In the literature, this problem has rarely been considered and never been solved; yet modern sociology has assembled all the tools for its solution.

The meaning of expressions like "social norms," "role expectations defined by society," and "sanctions imposed by society" cannot be explained in general terms except by metaphors or demonstrably unsatisfactory statements.[20] Does "society" in such expressions mean all people in a given society? This interpretation is obviously too broad. Most people in any given society play no part whatever, direct or indirect, in formulating the expectations that make up such roles as father, grammar school teacher, and citizen (to say nothing of treasurer of the X-town soccer club or vice-chairman of the local branch of the Y party). They are not asked, and even if they were, their opinion would have little binding force for others. Whatever the significance of opinion surveys may be, no one claims that they are the source of norms. Is it then perhaps a country's parliament or government that specifies role expectations and sanctions on behalf of "society"? Clearly this assumption is not altogether wrong, but it is too narrow. Even in a totalitarian state, at least shall- and can-expectations defy administrative commands; and in any state many norms of social behavior are unknown, and indeed of no interest, to the government. Where approaches of this sort go wrong is in trying to relate the singular noun "society" to a single agency or collectivity, and thus ignoring the possibility that society might conceal a multitude of forces of similar character but diverse origins.

In defining position and role, we observed that it is sometimes useful to regard both categories as sets of segments. Most positions involve not merely a single relation to another person (such as husband-wife), but a field of relations to other persons and to categories or aggregates of persons. The grammar school teacher is linked to his pupils, their parents, his colleagues, and his superiors, and he recognizes a separate, identifiable set of expectations for each of these groups. He is supposed to impart knowledge to his pupils but not to his superiors, to decide on his pupils' marks with colleagues but not with parents. If he is unfriendly to his colleagues, he incurs

---

[20] The same holds for expressions in which "social" and "society" do not explicitly appear, such as "institutionalized expectations" and "culture patterns." All such expressions require precise definition, at least with respect to social roles.

their sanctions, not those of his pupils; and whether he shows deference to his superiors is a matter of little concern to his pupils' parents. It seems plausible to think of "society" with respect to this
position in terms of the groups that make up its relational field:
i.e., to explore the connection between the norms of these groups
and the role expectations of the positions defined by them.

In interpreting the data gathered in the United States by Samuel
A. Stouffer and others about the American soldier in the Second
World War, Robert K. Merton developed the category of "reference group," which several social scientists have since found useful
for defining the notion of role.[21] This category, which originated
in social psychology and is used by Merton primarily in a social-
psychology sense, derives from the observation that people orient
their behavior according to the approval or disapproval of groups
to which they do not themselves belong. Reference groups are out-
groups functioning as value standards; they constitute the frame of
reference within which a person evaluates his own behavior and
that of others. With only a slight narrowing and shift of meaning
the concept may be interpreted sociologically and applied to our
present problems. If we define a reference group not as an arbi-
trarily chosen out-group, but as a group to which a person has a
necessary relation by virtue of one of his social positions, we can
state that every position segment establishes a relation between the
position's incumbent and one or more reference groups. Thus understood, reference groups are of course not necessarily out-groups;
the incumbent may be a member of such a group by virtue of his
position. In these terms, the position field of teacher Schmidt may
be described as an aggregate of reference groups every one of which
imposes prescriptions on him and is capable of sanctioning his behavior either positively or negatively. The question of the nature of
"society" turns into another question: How do reference groups

---

[21] Merton first developed this category in his essay "Contributions to the Theory
of Reference Group Behavior," written with Alice S. Rossi. He later elaborated it in
a longer essay, "Continuities in the Theory of Reference Groups and Social Structure"
(see 4). The theory of reference groups has been related to role analysis by Merton
himself, as well as by Joseph Ben-David, David Mandelbaum, Siegfried F. Nadel, and
others.

formulate and sanction the expectations of the positions they define?[22]

To my knowledge, a similar question has been raised only once in the literature, in Neal Gross *et al.*, *Explorations in Role Analysis* (13). The answer offered by Gross and his coauthors warrants a brief departure from our strategy of deferring a critical examination of the literature. Gross distinguishes as we do between positions and roles, and conceives them both as aggregates of segments. For Gross as for us, every position segment and role segment refers to a group of other positions and roles (he does not use the term "reference group"). As a way of discovering exactly how these reference groups influence the positions and roles that they define, Gross suggests asking the members of a given position's reference groups what expectations they associate with the position's incumbent. Gross himself applied this suggestion to the position of school superintendent. In a series of interviews, he asked superintendents' superiors, teachers, superintendents themselves, and others what they expected from a school superintendent. Gross believed that their answers would help him to arrive at a clear definition of role expectations, and at the same time would indicate to what extent the members of a reference group agree with respect to such expectations. Unsurprisingly, on many points Gross found no consensus at all, or at best a weak majority. He is accordingly moved to ask:

How much consensus on what behaviors is required for a society to maintain itself? How much disagreement can a society tolerate in what areas? To what extent do different sets of role definers hold the same role definitions of key positions in a society? On what aspects of role definitions do members of different "subcultures" in a society agree and disagree? To what extent is deviant behavior a function of deviant role definitions?

---

[22] Obviously the concept of "group" is used in a very loose sense when one speaks of reference groups. At least in the modified meaning that we have given the concept here, reference groups are not only groups proper, i.e. identifiable formal units, but also, among other things, mere categories like "inhabitants of town X." It is rarely a good idea to extend a term's meaning this way. If Merton had not reserved the term "role-set" for a slightly (although not entirely) different meaning (see 24), we might consider using "reference sets" rather than "reference groups."

Why do members of society differ in their role definitions? (13: 31.)

In more than one respect, the study by Gross and his coauthors represents an advance over earlier discussions of role. It is conceptually clear and plausible; above all, it makes a serious attempt to replace "society" by more precise and operationally useful categories. But in seeking to relate his concepts to empirical research, Gross abandons one of the essential elements of the category of social role. By attributing the force of social norms to the uncertain basis of majority opinions, he makes the fact of society subject to the arbitrariness of questionnaire responses. If six out of ten parents interviewed think that a school superintendent should not smoke and should be married, these expected attributes or actions are for Gross constituents of the role of school superintendent; if, on the other hand—Gross does not go this far, but nothing in his approach rules out such absurdities—thirty-five out of forty pupils think that none of them should ever get bad marks, this too is an expectation, associated in the first instance with the role of teacher but applying also to the school superintendent as the teacher's superior.

One suspects that Gross has taken the word "expectation" too literally, and has forgotten that laws also involve expectations by which people's behavior is guided into certain channels, indeed that laws and law courts are outstanding examples of what is meant by role expectations and sanctions. Role expectations are not modes of behavior about whose desirability there is a more or less impressive consensus; they are modes of behavior that are binding for the individual and whose binding character is institutionalized, i.e., valid independently of his own or anybody else's opinion.[23] It follows that if we are to connect the categories of role and reference group, it will not be by ascertaining the opinions of reference group

[23] In this respect Gross misunderstands earlier role definitions when he imputes to them a "postulate of role consensus" (13: chap. iii). Imprecise as it may be to speak of "culture patterns" and "expectations defined by society," such phrases clearly imply quasi-objective, institutionalized norms, not a consensus of opinions or conceptions. What must be rendered precise, therefore, is norms and not opinions.

members. If there is any point in interviews of this sort, it is to find out what prescriptions and sanctions are in fact valid in these groups, and constitute, so to speak, their "positive law."

Our thesis here is that the agency which defines a given position's role expectations and sanctions may be found in the norms and sanctions of that position's reference groups, and specifically in such of these norms and sanctions as refer to the position in question. Grammar school teacher Schmidt is a state official, and is therefore subject to the general statutes pertaining to officials and the special regulations of his department; he is a teacher, and is thus subject to the rules and prescriptions of his professional organization; but on a less formal level his pupils and their parents also constitute reference groups with defined norms and sanctions aimed at teachers' behavior. Generally speaking, it is possible to identify in any human group those rules and sanctions by which it influences the behavior of its members and of those non-members with whom it establishes relations. These rules and sanctions, which can in principle be separated from the opinions of both members and non-members, are the origin of role expectations and of their binding character. It follows that to articulate these expectations for a given position, we must first identify the position's reference groups and then find out what norms obtain in these groups with respect to that particular position.

Obviously, such a procedure works best with organized reference groups. All must- and most shall-expectations of social positions are the work of such groups. Must-expectations are found only where society as a whole, through its legal system, is the relevant reference group, i.e., where certain demands on the incumbent of a position are enforced by law. Shall-expectations often have their origin in public organizations or institutions, professional associations, business enterprises, political parties, or clubs, many of which have by-laws, or clearly established customs or precedents, that spell out their norms and sanctions. But when we come to a reference group like "pupils' parents," and in general to the whole range of uncodified can-expectations, documents and precedents do not help us much. Is it not, after all, essential in this case to interview members of reference groups and seek a consensus? Sensible and realistic as this method may seem, it is nevertheless fallacious. If we want to preserve the concept of role from the arbitrariness of individual opinions, to keep it at the point of intersection of the individual and society, it is far better to forget about can-expectations for the time being than to substitute the behavioral pseudo-precision of opinion research for the structural fruitfulness of the category of role. Since adequate methods for identifying unfixed role expectations have not yet been found, we shall accordingly confine ourselves to formulating the accessible elements of social roles in terms of known norms, customs, and precedents.[24]

The opinions of the members of reference groups and the degree of consensus in these groups are obviously significant both for sociometric purposes and for role analysis. But their significance is not where Gross presumed to find it. So far we have taken the norms and sanctions of the reference groups of social positions as given; but it remains to ask how these norms came into being as such in the first place, or—what is the same thing—how they can be changed or repealed. Possibly there is an analogy between consensus and norms on the one hand, and custom and law on the other. A norm that is not supported or at least tolerated by a majority of group members is on weak ground. If, for example, a teachers' association requires all teachers to arrange weekly parents' meetings but most teachers consider it pointless to hold meetings so frequently, we can safely predict that in due course this norm will be modified, or at least that it will not be enforced and will thus be converted from a shall- into a can-expectation. It is not the validity of norms but their legitimacy that is affected by the opinions of those concerned: thus if Gross had weighed the findings of his study against the institutionalized role expectations of the position of school superintendent, he might have come up with some interesting findings

---

[24] In informal groupings, such as the parents of a given teacher's pupils, norms often become visible only if challenged (and then, of course, in intimate contact with the opinions of those involved). A teacher tells his pupils obvious nonsense, which they relay to their parents; the parents decide to do something about it. Such precedents then live on as norms; where they are present, we can identify can-expectations. For a possible alternative way of identifying can-expectations, as for the whole problem of the empirical analysis of role expectations, see section VIII below.

about the future of this role and the legitimacy of the associated expectations. In a theoretical discussion, then, we must distinguish clearly between (1) fixed norms of reference groups, which are assigned to the incumbent of a position as role expectations; (2) the opinions of members of reference groups about these norms, which determine their legitimacy and likelihood of change; and (3) the actual behavior of role players. For the concept of social role, norms are relevant only in the first sense, as expectations; questions about their legitimacy and the actual behavior of the persons to whom they apply presuppose the role concept and are significant only in terms of that concept.

Among the reference groups that have us all, as incumbents of social positions, in their sway, society as a whole with its legal system is of particular interest, among other things because of its apparent resemblance to the "society" that we have dismissed as too imprecise a concept for sociological analysis. We have defined must-expectations as expectations supported by the force of law and the sanctions of law courts. Wherever these expectations apply, it is clear that no subdivision of society can be identified as the appropriate reference group. Although not all parts of the legal system are applicable to us in every one of our roles—although civil-service law is irrelevant to father Schmidt, and maritime law to Herr Schmidt in all his roles—neither the legal system as a whole nor any of its parts may be described as a norm instituted for others by a particular reference group. As a set of latent expectations, or more frequently prohibitions, the law applies to us in most of our social roles. Insofar as teacher Schmidt is subject to civil-service law and father Schmidt to family law, we must assume that the whole society of which Herr Schmidt is a part measures his behavior in terms of these norms. Here "the whole society" means all members of society to the extent that they are represented by legislative and judiciary institutions. In this limited sense, society as a whole constitutes a reference group, and functions like other reference groups in defining and controlling role expectations.[25]

[25] This raises difficult problems that cannot be explored here. Their core is the fact that maritime law, for example, although applicable only to a limited set of persons and institutions, involves as law the claim to universality. In empirical analy-

Unless appearances deceive, applying reference group theory to the category of social role can help us to replace the personification "society" by more precise categories. With respect to social roles, the vexatious fact of society proves to be a conglomeration of more or less binding, more or less particular group norms. Every group contributes to determining the patterns of many roles; conversely, every role may be the result of influences from many groups. The resulting pattern is not always a unified, well-balanced whole; indeed, it may be characterized by various forms of social conflict, among them conflict within roles, which we shall consider below. What happens when the norms of teacher Schmidt's colleagues and those of his superiors prescribe contradictory behavior for him, so that whatever he does will disappoint one group or the other and incur its sanctions? Some conflicts of this kind are notorious in modern societies. One thinks of the university professor, torn between the demands of research, teaching, and administration; of the doctor, torn between doing his best to help his patients and charging as little as possible to the public health insurance; of the labor manager in a co-determination enterprise, torn between cooperating with his managerial colleagues and serving the workers he represents. These examples suggest how conceptual clarification, by enabling us to ask more precise questions, may contribute to the solution of empirical problems.

VI

In the last two sections we tried to elucidate the "binding character" and "social definition" of role expectations. Another idea that needs explaining takes the form of statements such as "Roles are assigned to the individual," or "In roles, the individual and society are mediated." How does a person acquire his positions and roles, and how does he relate to them? Since sociologists have de-

---

sis, this double aspect of laws is further obscured by special-interest legislation, laws pushed through parliaments by particular groups who seek to give their norms the appearance of universality. In terms of logic, it is important to recognize that as a reference group "society as a whole" need not be regarded as comprising all other groups, but may in given contexts stand alongside other reference groups as a subset of itself.

voted considerable attention to these questions, our discussion here becomes to a great extent a summary of familiar research. At the same time, this discussion will bring us very close to the initial problem of this essay: the problem of how to state clearly, and how to make bearable, the paradoxical relationship between the human being of our experience and role-playing *homo sociologicus*. For the relationship of the individual to his social roles involves the creation of *homo sociologicus* out of his human counterpart, the transformation of man into an actor on the stage of society.

The encounter of individual and society can be clarified by an intellectual experiment which, though clearly unrealistic, offers insights of considerable value. Since positions can be conceived and related to each other independently of their occupants, the structure of society can be thought of as a giant organization chart in which millions of positions are centered in their fields like suns with their planet systems. Grammar school teacher, father, German, and treasurer of the X-town soccer club are all places on this chart that can be identified without so much as thinking of Herr Schmidt. Next, let us imagine that Herr Schmidt and all his contemporaries are as yet devoid of any social position, that they represent pure social potential. The intellectual experiment consists in devising ways of joining the two, the positions on the chart and the position-less people, in such a way that every position on the chart is occupied by at least one person and every person is given at least one position. The latter requirement is easier to satisfy than the former, for the number of positions far exceeds the number of available people; but nearly random combinations of positions should be permitted.[26] Less schematically, but analogously in the points that concern us, every society is faced with the task of bringing together positions and men; this is one basic function of the social process.[27] Mathe-

[26] In social reality, of course, the possibilities of combining positions and people are by no means random. Rather, it would seem possible to develop a classification of positions so that every person can have but one position in every class (e.g., the classes of sex, age, family, national, and occupational positions). This is the difference between the fact of society and purely random conditions.

[27] The process of position allocation is often described by English and American sociologists as one of role allocation. If one accepts the distinction between positions and roles suggested here, the expression is imprecise; for what is allocated is in the first place positions (although each position has an associated role).

matically speaking, the problem of coordinating a great many "persons" with even more "positions" has a huge number of possible solutions. With respect to individual positions and persons, the same holds for society. But among these solutions, groups may be distinguished by certain criteria, and social mechanisms may be indicated that lead to certain solutions. Just as the behavior of *homo sociologicus* does not simply follow the laws of random probability, so the process of position allocation is not a matter of unrestricted mathematical permutations.

With respect to allocation, social positions are of two broad types: those that a person can do nothing about one way or the other, and those that he acquires by his own activity. All positions based on biological characteristics, for example, are of the first type: Herr Schmidt's sex and age positions (the fact that he is a man and an adult) are no more within his power to alter than his position as son in his family of origin. That he is a German and a citizen also follows automatically from the fact that he was born in a certain place and has reached a certain age. In addition to these *ascribed positions*, however, Herr Schmidt as a German in the middle of the twentieth century has a number of *achieved positions,* i.e., positions that he occupies at least to some extent by his own effort. In becoming a grammar school teacher, treasurer of the soccer club, and a driver, he has asserted an element of choice; these positions have not fallen to him without effort on his part. The distinction between ascribed and achieved positions is valid for all societies; but positions may change from ascribed to achieved, and (more rarely) vice versa. The "occupational" position of king in a hereditary monarchy is not achieved, and the same was true of many other occupations in preindustrial societies. Indeed, the distinction between these ascribed and achieved positions is not always clear. Is "Catholic" for the child of Catholic parents in a Catholic country an achieved position? Is "father" for Herr Schmidt an ascribed position? If we take the realistic possiblity of choice as our standard, we must answer no in both cases; but even this criterion cannot exclude marginal cases.[28]

[28] The distinction between ascribed and achieved positions was introduced in this meaning by Ralph Linton (19: 115): "Ascribed statuses are those which are assigned

Ascribed positions are like the prescriptions of a totally planned economy; society need not concern itself with their destiny. Indeed, to be quite rigorous we should have to exclude these positions from our intellectual experiment as being not generally available. With achieved positions, by contrast, where individual choice is involved, some social mechanism is necessary to decide who acquires which positions. Not everybody can become prime minister, president of a company, or treasurer of the X-town soccer club. In industrial societies the educational system tends to be the decisive social mechanism for assigning achieved positions (if the paradox is permitted), at least insofar as these may be broadly described as occupations. In schools and universities the individual's choice is brought into line with society's various needs for achievement; the diploma translates the resulting performance into a claim to a certain kind or level of achieved position. Within social organizations, too, the principle of achievement (activity, success) serves as a criterion for allocating positions. But as a result of these institutional mechanisms for evaluating achievement, the allocation of positions becomes a process of permanently decreasing possibilities, and further constants are introduced into our mathematical experiment. Even the ascribed position "man" limits the sum of all further possible positions; such positions as adult, professional man, and inhabitant of town X are further restrictions. Eventually, such restrictions reduce Herr Schmidt's range of choice to such an extent that only a very limited number of positions remain open for him. Here again it is but a step from experiencing society as a support and a source of security to experiencing it as an obstacle and a vexation.

In any case, social positions are a Danaän gift from society to the individual. Even if he has not acquired them by his own effort, even if they have been ascribed to him from birth, they demand something from him; for every position carries with it a social role, a set

---

to individuals without reference to their innate differences or abilities. They can be predicted and trained for from the moment of birth. The achieved statuses are, as a minimum, those requiring special qualities, although they are not necessarily limited to these. They are not assigned to individuals from birth, but are left open to be filled through competition and individual effort." Even apart from the term "status" (on which see section VII), this definition contains a number of obscure features that have only recently been cleared up along the lines indicated in the text.

of expectations addressed to the behavior of its incumbent and sanctioned by the reference groups of its field. But before the individual can play his roles, he must know them; like an actor, man as a social being must learn his roles, become familiar with their substance and the sanctions that enforce them. Here we encounter a second basic mechanism of society, the process of socialization by the internalizing of behavior patterns. The individual must somehow take into himself the prescriptions of society and make them the basis of his behavior; it is by this means that the individual and society are mediated and man is reborn as *homo sociologicus*. Position allocation and role internalization are complementary, and it is thus no accident that industrial societies have assigned primary responsibility for both processes to a single institutional order— the educational system. Even in modern societies, however, the family, the church, and other institutions support the educational system in its task of allocating positions and socializing the young.

The two concepts generally used to describe the process of mediation between the totally unsocial individual and a completely individuated society—socialization and internalization—clearly belong to the point of intersection between the individual and society; and the category of role accordingly falls on the borderline of sociology and psychology.[29] From the point of view of society and sociology, it is by learning role expectations, by being transformed into *homo sociologicus,* that man becomes a part of society and accessible to sociological analysis. Man devoid of roles is a nonentity for society and sociology. To become a part of society and a subject of sociological analysis, man must be socialized, chained to the fact of society

[29] The intermediate position of role between sociology and psychology is often emphasized, and is indeed an important characteristic of role. A remark by Bertrand Russell is apposite here: "Every account of structure is relative to certain units which are, for the time being, treated as if they were devoid of structure, but it must never be assumed that these units will not, in another context, have a structure which it is important to recognize." (37: 269.) For the sociologist, roles are irreducible elements of analysis. The psychologist, by contrast, is concerned with their other, inner side, the side facing the individual, and he is accordingly led to dissolve roles into their psychologically relevant components. A systematic delimitation of the two disciplines in these terms would be conceivable, but like other such delimitations it would be of doubtful utility.

and made its creature. By observation, imitation, indoctrination, and conscious learning, he must grow into the forms that society holds in readiness for him as an incumbent of positions. His parents, friends, teachers, priests, and superiors are important to society above all as agents who cut into his social *tabula rasa* the plan of his life in society. If society is interested in the family, the school, and the church, it is only partly because they help the individual to develop his talents fully; it is primarily because they prepare him effectively and economically for carrying out all the tasks that society has set him.

For society and sociology, socialization invariably means depersonalization, the yielding up of man's absolute individuality and liberty to the constraint and generality of social roles. Man become *homo sociologicus* is exposed without protection to the laws of society and the hypotheses of sociology. The process occurs wherever society exists. Only Robinson Crusoe can hope to prevent his alienated rebirth as *homo sociologicus.*

For the individual and for psychology this process has a different aspect. From this perspective human beings are not transformed into something alien, are not socialized; rather, they take something that exists outside them into themselves, internalize it, and make it a part of their personality. By learning to play social roles, then, we not only lose ourselves to the alien otherness of a world we never made, but regain ourselves as personalities given unique shape by that world's vexations. At least for the psychology of personality, the internalization of role expectations is one of the significant formative processes of human life; as we know from recent research, it simultaneously affects many levels of the personality. It may increase our knowledge, or it may lead to repressions and conflicts; in any case, it affects us very deeply. Socially, the most important corollary of the internalization of social roles is the concurrent internalization of the sanctions which, as custom and law, control our behavior. Since Freud, it has been clear that the norms of society and other reference groups can be to some extent internalized in the conscience or superego, with the result that the warning and sentencing voice of society is capable of sanctioning our behavior through ourselves. At least for some roles and role expectations, we can assume that external agencies are not necessary to remind us of the binding character of social statutes. It is by no means unimportant that society can judge our behavior by our own conscience even where we succeed in deceiving the policeman or the judge.

Beyond all psychology and sociology, the vexation of society is a question of how much freedom of choice is left to man by the all-pervading constraints of society, or—to put the question more actively—how much he can arrogate to himself. In its most frightening aspect the world of *homo sociologicus* is a "brave new world" or a "1984," a society in which all human behavior has become calculable, predictable, and subject to permanent control. In reality, however, although we are in fact unable to separate Herr Schmidt from the role player Schmidt, after all his roles are taken into account he retains a residual range of choice that escapes calculation and control. It is not easy to define this range of choice, but it appears to have at least three components. There is not only the freedom that every role leaves its player by not pronouncing on certain matters (for example, father Schmidt's free choice of playing ball or playing electric trains), but also a freedom *within* role expectations arising from the fact that they are largely defined by exclusion rather than determined positively. Few role expectations are all-encompassing prescriptions; most take the form of a range of permitted deviations. Expectations associated with negative sanctions, in particular, are essentially privative; we are not supposed to do certain things, but are otherwise free to do as we please. Finally, the individual's alienated relationship to society implies that he both is and is not society; if society shapes his personality, he can help shape society. Role expectations and sanctions are not unalterably fixed for all time; like everything social they can be changed by changes in people's behavior and opinions. However, much as such considerations may do toward reconciling us to the paradox of *homo sociologicus*, they scarcely help to render *homo sociologicus* more compatible with the man of our everyday experience.

VII

Only in a meaninglessly general sense can we say that *homo sociologicus,* as we have sketched him here, is at the basis of all theoretical and empirical research in contemporary sociology. There has been an unmistakable trend toward agreement on the meaning and importance of social position and role, and on the use of these specific terms; but there remain astonishing differences between sociologists with respect to these and other elements of sociological analysis, as the merest glance through any sociological journal will confirm. This is one of the reasons why we have put off discussing earlier attempts to describe the man of sociology. At last, however, we are in a position not only to summarize recent work on roles and deride it as full of contradictions, as is usually done,[30] but to resolve the contradictions by considered critical decisions. In doing so, we shall confine ourselves to a few main aspects of the conceptual dispute, and a few of the leading disputants. We can accordingly claim only representativeness, and not completeness, for the positions and problems discussed.

The terminologically strict use of the elementary categories in question here can be traced to Ralph Linton's discussion of "Status and Role" in his *Study of Man,* which first appeared in 1936. Nearly all later attempts at definition cite this discussion, and although Linton himself later modified his views—whether intentionally or unintentionally is not clear—it seems sensible to start with what he originally wrote.[31] Linton first speaks of "status," which is what we have called "position" here: "A status, in the abstract, is a position in a particular pattern." (19: 113.) This definition, which is similar to ours but less precise, Linton immediately elaborates as follows: "A status, as distinct from the individual who may occupy

---

[30] Such summaries have been published at regular intervals; see, for example, those by L. J. Neiman and J. W. Hughes (29), Theodore R. Sarbin (38), and Neal Gross *et al.* (13).

[31] On Linton's later changes, see Gross *et al.* (13: 12–13), and note 36 below.

it, is simply a collection of rights and duties." (19 : 113.) By way of illustration Linton uses the much-quoted image of the driver's seat in a car: the car's equipment—steering wheel, gearshift, accelerator, brakes, clutch—is given to the individual driver as a constant with equal potential for all drivers. How then are roles defined? "A role represents the dynamic aspect of a status. The individual is socially assigned to a status and occupies it with relation to other statuses. When he puts the rights and duties which constitute the status into effect, he is performing a role. Role and status are quite inseparable, and the distinction between them is of only academic interest." (19: 114.)

Few statements by sociologists have been quoted as often as these sentences, and yet all the ambiguities of the categories "role" and "status" (or "position") are present in this, their classic definition. The first ambiguity is terminological: we must establish terms for the two elementary categories that are not only adequate but reasonably unlikely to be misunderstood. Like all terminological questions, this is of but moderate substantive significance. The second ambiguity is in the delimitation of the two categories, if indeed (considering Linton's last remark) two categories are necessary at all. This ambiguity is rather more significant than the first. If status describes a "collection of rights and duties," what remains for role? Is there a substantively justified, formulable difference between the "static" and "dynamic" aspects of places in a field of social relations?[32] These questions consistently lead to a third ambiguity both in Linton's definition and in most later ones, an ambiguity that has occupied us before and requires special attention. Are roles what the individual does with patterns given to him by society, or are they as much a part of society as they are of the individual? Are they objective data, separable from the individual, or subjective ones, inseparably part of his personal life?

---

[32] "Static" and "dynamic" are expressions that sociologists use often and with pleasure; yet they rarely have an unambiguous meaning. In the present context they seem to me entirely out of place. In what sense are my "rights" more static than my "actions"? Why is my position more static than my "rights"? Unfortunately, as some of the following quotations show, not only Linton's definition but his distinction between "static" and "dynamic" roles has survived for a generation.

This last ambiguity raises the most important problems, as we shall see. Linton himself seems to understand by roles not complexes of expected modes of behavior (which he ascribes instead to "status" as "rights and duties"), but actual behavior with respect to such expectations. Seen this way, "role" is not a quasi-objective elementary category of sociology, a category in principle independent of specific individuals, but a variable of social psychology. How teacher Schmidt in fact behaves to his pupils or his superiors is by no means without social interest, but it tells us less about the fact of society than about Herr Schmidt's personality. This error, which is not fully articulated by Linton, is carried to its logical conclusion by Kingsley Davis when he says:

How an individual actually performs in a given position, as distinct from how he is supposed to perform, we call his role. The role, then, is the manner in which a person actually carries out the requirements of his position. It is the dynamic aspect of status or office and as such is always influenced by factors other than the stipulations of the position itself. (9: 89–90.)

Here, the category of role is almost deliberately removed from the area of intersection between the individual and society and handed over to the social psychologist. So defined, role fails to incorporate precisely what we had regarded as central to it, namely behavior expectations. The approach of Hans H. Gerth and C. Wright Mills is very similar: "More technically, the concept of 'role' refers to units of conduct (1) which by their recurrence stand out as regularities and (2) which are oriented to the conduct of other actors." (12: 10.) If sociologists define role in this way, one can hardly blame social psychologists for distinguishing with H. A. Murray between "individual roles" and "social roles" (25: 450–51), or for agreeing with P. R. Hofstätter: "As a role one may define a coherent behavior sequence which is geared to the behavior sequences of other persons." (14: 36.) (In fact Hofstätter, who speaks a little later of the "separability of roles from their particular bearer," is more sociological than the sociologists quoted.) People's regular behavior toward other people gains sociological meaning only insofar as it may be understood as behavior with respect to predetermined patterns that are assigned to the incumbent of a social position irrespective of his individual identity. It is these patterns, and not (as with Linton, Davis, Gerth and Mills, and many social psychologists) the behavior itself, that we have called social roles.

Psychologizing definitions characterize one line of thinking about the category of role. A second, which surprisingly never conflicts openly with the first, has been much more fruitful. It is especially surprising that George C. Homans and Talcott Parsons, both of whom explicitly refer to Linton's definition, do not apparently see it as conflicting with their own much less ambiguous and indeed very different formulations: "A norm that states the expected relationship of a person in a certain position to others he comes into contact with is often called the role of this person." (Homans, 16: 124.) "The role is that organized sector of an actor's orientation which constitutes and defines his participation in an interactive process. It involves a set of complementary expectations concerning his own actions and those of others with whom he interacts." (Parsons, 32: 23.) Similarly, John W. Bennett and Melvin M. Tumin understand by roles "the expected behavior which goes along with the occupancy of a status" (5: 96), and Merton speaks of "structurally defined expectations assigned to each role" (24: 110). All these characterizations of role are based on the objectivated, sociological notion of complexes of expected behavior, as opposed to actual regularities of behavior.

These two concepts of role are clearly incompatible. The first defines Herr Schmidt's father role as the way he regularly behaves toward his children; the second finds it in the norms that his society has generally adopted and laid down for fathers. T. H. Marshall, perceiving the difficulty, has proposed that the two approaches be reconciled by leaving the category of role entirely to social psychology and making status, purged of its psychological elements, the basis of sociological analysis: "Status emphasizes the position as conceived by the group or society that sustains it. . . . Status emphasizes the fact that expectations (of a normative kind) exist in the relevant social groups." (21: 13.) To support his proposal, Marshall cites the legal definition of status as a "condition of belonging to a particular class of persons to whom the law assigns peculiar legal capacities or incapacities, or both" (21: 15). Siegfried F. Nadel also invokes the legal concept of status: "By status I shall mean the rights and obligations of any individual relative both to those of others and to the scale of worthwhileness valid in the group." (27: 171.) However, contrary to Marshall's proposal and following A. R. Radcliffe-Brown, Nadel introduces the parallel concept of "person," a term that we have encountered in a similar meaning in the "persona" of the drama.[33] As a last example of the attempt to achieve terminological clarity by extending the concept of status, we offer Chester I. Barnard's definition of status as "that condition of the individual that is defined by a statement of his rights, privileges, immunities, duties, obligations . . . and, obversely, by a statement of the restrictions, limitations, and prohibitions governing his behavior, both determining the expectations of others in reference thereto" (3: 47–48).

Confusing as the abundance of definitions may appear, they clearly have a common core very near the assumptions of our earlier discussion. All the authors cited assume an elementary category of sociological analysis that is defined by expected patterns of behavior ("rights and duties"); apart from Continental European sociology, which in this respect as in others is still hampered by a provincialism stemming from its older but outdated traditions,[34] there are hardly

[33] Cf. Radcliffe-Brown: "The components or units of social structure are persons, and a person is a human being considered not as an organism but as occupying a position in a social structure." (36: 9-10.) "Within an organization each person may be said to have a role. . . ." (36: 11.) Nadel: "We might here speak of different 'aspects' of a person, or of different 'roles' assumed by it, or simply of different 'persons.' Though this is a question of words, the last-named usage seems to me the most consistent as well as convenient one. Understood in this sense, the person is more than the individual; it is the individual with certain recognized, or institutionalized, tasks and relationships, and is all the individuals who act in this way." (28: 93.) In a footnote to this remark Nadel refers to the close connection of the concepts "person" and "status" in legal language. But it is clear both from Nadel's formulations and from Radcliffe-Brown's that the category of "person" is too inclusive to replace that of position or of role; their concept of "person" corresponds rather to our *homo sociologicus*.

[34] This statement was truer when this essay was written (in 1957) than it is today. After becoming familiar with the work of sociologists in other countries, European

any differences of opinion on this point. Most of the authors cited propose a pair of such categories: either "status" and "role" (following Linton); or "position" or "office" and "role" (Homans, Davis); or "status" and "person" (Nadel). Even those authors who propose only the single category of "status" seem in effect to recognize two categories. Marshall, for example, in defining status simultaneously as position and as a complex of normative expectations, ascribes to one concept two quite distinct meanings. Marshall's definition shows at least the possibility, if not the necessity, of distinguishing between a place in a field of social relations and the expectations associated with occupying this place. Quite apart from the question of which terms may prove most suitable, the definitions quoted suggest that we need not one concept, but two.

Finally, a psychological element appears in some definitions, namely, the actual behavior of the individual incumbents of positions. Now it is indeed one of the tasks of sociology "to provide the link between the structural study of social systems and the psychological study of personality and motivation" (Marshall, 21: 11), but precisely this connecting-link function makes it necessary to guard jealously the intermediate position of sociology's basic categories. There is no way to get from what the individual does, or even does regularly, to the fact of society, which in principle is independent of the individual. The sum and the average of individual actions are as incapable of explaining the reality of law and custom as a consensus ascertained by interviews. Society is a fact, and a vexatious one at that, precisely because it is created neither by our impulses nor by our habitual behavior. I can break the rules of my reference groups, and I can break a long-standing habit; but the two kinds of action are essentially incommensurate. The first puts me into a tangible conflict with the fact of society, a force outside myself; the second involves only myself. The behavior of *homo sociologicus*, of man at the point of intersection between the individual and society, cannot be determined by "factors other than those given with the position," as Davis rightly states in discussing the effects of actual

---

sociologists have at last begun again to contribute actively to the theoretical discussion in the discipline.

behavior, without recognizing that by this standard his own role concept becomes sociologically useless. The person of our everyday experience expresses himself by individual variations of behavior; not so *homo sociologicus*.

Leaving aside all psychological elements, then, we may summarize the present state of the problem as follows. Some authors use a single term, usually "status," to describe both a place in a field of relations and the expectations associated with this place; with these authors, as with Linton, "status" oscillates in meaning between "position" and "rights and duties." Other authors use two terms, often "status" and "role," to express these two meanings. (Interestingly enough, some authors have tended to fuse both meanings in the term "role"; thus Parsons, for example, who used the term "status-role-bundle" in his writings before 1951, has since spoken mostly of "roles.") Reduced to these terms, the old conceptual dispute turns largely into a terminological question, which is to say a matter to be determined by considerations of convenience. We need only make a simple critical decision to escape the maze of definitions and counterdefinitions without injury to the basic ideas of any of the conflicting parties.

Fortunately, terminological clarification requires only a short step in a familiar direction. As the term for a place in a field of social relations, "status" and "position" compete for recognition. But "status" is losing ground, and for good reason. In general usage, "status" refers primarily to one particular kind of position, namely, position in a hierarchical scale of social prestige, a meaning that differs significantly from the one in question here.[35] The same holds for the word's legal meaning. Legal status means more than merely a place in a network of relations; indeed, it includes certain rights and duties that we specifically want to separate from the simple concept of place. "Position," by contrast, is a neutral word, unburdened by misleading connotations, which is exactly what we

---

[35] Strictly speaking, "social status" in this sense describes not only a special kind of position, but a position of positions. Not a human being, but a position (e.g. an occupation) has prestige and in that sense a "status." This meaning of "status," which is important in many contexts, must be distinguished clearly from our much more neutral concept of position.

need. In using "position" we have followed the lead of Gross and his colleagues.[36]

As for "role," the term itself is generally accepted; the problem, as we have seen, is that social psychologists and sociologists assign it different meanings. If neither discipline is prepared to renounce the term, a definitive solution may be impossible in the foreseeable future. And yet it appears that the divergence of definitions may be more apparent than real. As it happens, social psychologists have succeeded in rendering the notion of habitual behavior precise, whereas sociologists have so far failed to do the same with their notion of expected behavior. Once this deficiency is remedied, I see no reason why the concept and term "social role" should not be accepted by social scientists in the sense indicated in this essay.

Our critical survey of the literature in this section has been rather more general and vague than the discussions of previous sections. Unfortunately, this corresponds to the state of the problem. Only in the works of Gross and Merton do we find impressive advances in rendering the fundamental categories of sociological analysis more precise. With their distinction between roles and role segments, or role sets and roles, these authors have cleared the way for connecting role theory and reference group theory, and have helped prepare the way for the empirical investigation of roles.[37]

---

[36] Linton's arguments against this use of "position" are incomprehensible to me. They are nonetheless of interest as illustrating Linton's later thoughts on the elementary categories in question: "The place in a particular system which a certain individual occupies at a particular time will be referred to as his status with respect to that system. The term position has been used by some other students of social structure in much the same sense, but without clear recognition of the time factor or of the existence of simultaneous systems of organization within the society. Status has long been used with reference to the position of an individual in the prestige system of a society. In the present usage this is extended to apply to his position in each of the other systems. The second term, role, will be used to designate the sum total of the culture patterns associated with a particular status. It thus includes the attitudes, values, and behavior ascribed by the society to any and all persons occupying this status. It can even be extended to include the legitimate expectations of such persons with respect to the behavior toward them of persons in other statuses within the same system.... Insofar as it represents overt behavior, a role is the dynamic aspect of a status: what the individual has to do in order to validate his occupation of the status." (20: 368.)

[37] Since this was written, some good work has been done along these lines, notably by Michael Banton (1), Siegfried F. Nadel (28), and Heinrich Popitz (35).

Although *homo sociologicus* was until recently a mere postulate, an idea whose usefulness many suspected but no one had conclusively demonstrated, there would seem to be a chance today of testing the postulate by applying it to empirical problems. Only after such a test proves successful will *homo sociologicus* change from a mere paradox of thought into a true doppelgänger, a disturbing approximation to the man of our experience. Only then will the alienated rebirth of man as *homo sociologicus* become an inescapable philosophical problem for sociologists.

VIII

The inventors of *homo oeconomicus* and psychological man did not conceive of them as embodying philosophies of human nature, although critics of these concepts have seen them as carrying this implication. If, as we have tried to show here, the critics' claim is not as easily dismissed as economists and psychologists would have us believe, still it has nothing to do with why these artificial men of social science were originally created. *Homo sociologicus* poses a dilemma that we can escape only by dogmatism; but it is not dogmatism that has led us to postulate the rebirth of man as a role-playing creature. Rather, it is the hope of making the fact of society accessible to statements whose validity can be decided by controlled observations. First of all, and above all else, *homo sociologicus* is a tool for rationalizing and explaining certain aspects of the world we live in. Scientific method in this sense has its own moral and philosophical problems. Very possibly tomorrow's sociologist will face as difficult a conflict of conscience as today's nuclear physicist.[38] But that must be as it will. To make a future Galileo of sociology publicly recant his insights would no more hold up the progress of sociology than Galileo's perjury held up the progress of physics. Obscurantism and suppression are always the worst means of deal-

[38] One need but think of the none too distant possibility of keeping totalitarian governments in power with the assistance of sociological insights—or of "human relations in industry," as the current phrase goes, whose implicit goal is often to prevent strikes and wage demands without regard to their legitimacy.

ing with imminent conflicts. Here as elsewhere it is better to face
the dilemma boldly than to run away from it.

In our discussion so far, the empirical or scientific usefulness of
homo sociologicus, the understanding we gain by his invention, has
been little more than an assertion, a promise. So far, published research bears out the promise only to a very limited extent.[39] At several points, we have hinted at possible applications of the role concept; we shall now incorporate these hints in a more systematic
argument for the usefulness of this concept in analyzing particular
sociological problems.

Categories like position, role, reference group, and sanction can
be applied to research problems only if they are operationally precise. We have referred several times to the difficulty of describing
particular social roles. Nearly everything remains to be done in this
respect. Ideally, the sociologist would have a kind of sociological
periodic table of elements at his disposal, i.e., an inventory or chart
showing all known positions with their associated role expectations
and sanctions (to begin with, perhaps, in one society). In fact, we
do not even have the beginnings of such an inventory; no strict description of a social role has ever been attempted.[40] It is not so much
that sociologists are indolent; it is rather that partial descriptions
of roles suffice for most problems of sociological analysis, and that
any description of social roles involves considerable methodological
and technical problems. Neither of these considerations, however,
relieves us of the necessity of developing adequate methods of describing social roles; for even partial descriptions, to be valid, presuppose such methods.

The first step in identifying social roles empirically is classifica-
tory. It seems sensible to begin by sorting out the classes of social

[39] Much as the concept of role has been discussed by sociologists, it is not used as
often in empirical research as one might expect; and where it is used, it is often
defined *ad hoc.* This disappointing situation is probably due in part to technical
difficulties (discussed below) in the way of rendering role and other categories empirically precise.

[40] Gross and his collaborators did of course intend to describe the role of the school
superintendent precisely (13). But their misleading definition of roles (by majority
opinions in reference groups) makes their description of little practical use.

positions that are applicable to everyone, or nearly everyone: e.g., the classes of family, occupational, national, class, age, and sex positions. Even if it should not make sense in the end to classify all known social positions, it seems possible and profitable (for example, in describing the positions held by a given person) to establish subdivisions for the most important classes of positions. We must also classify role expectations. Here we have made a beginning by distinguishing must-, shall-, and can-expectations; but more refined gradations are clearly desirable, perhaps even quantitative distinctions in the case of certain negative sanctions. A scale assigning numerical values to all possible negative sanctions from prison terms to disapproval by members of reference groups might be very useful in classifying role expectations.[41]

The next step is to identify the reference groups that define particular social positions. It is hard to say whether there is a determinate and determinable number of reference groups for any given position, but it would probably suffice to identify the most important reference groups for each position; often this information is readily inferrable from a position's place in an organizational or quasi-organizational context. What is hardest to assess is the relative weight of different reference groups for given positions. Who is more important for the role behavior of the teacher, his superiors or his colleagues?[42] Wherever two or more reference groups associate different expectations with a position, this question obviously becomes crucial. Perhaps it could be answered, and a rank order of reference groups established, on the basis of the severity of the negative sanctions at the disposal of the relevant reference groups.

The most important and most difficult step is to identify and define role expectations and sanctions. This is the difficulty on

---

[41] All standards are originally arbitrary; there is thus no reason why one should not try to classify sanctions, say, on a scale from 10 (long prison term) to 1 (disapproval by members of reference groups), or 0 (sanctionless role range). Such measures might also serve to distinguish groups of roles. For example, only a few roles extend into the range of severe sanctions (citizen, political positions); for this very reason these may well be of special significance.

[42] This question, too, must of course be understood as a structural question, i.e., a question of the importance of various reference groups in the institutional context, not of the personal preferences of a teacher or an average of teachers.

which all efforts to make the role concept operationally precise
have foundered. We have already indicated one way of overcoming
this difficulty, namely, by ascertaining all the laws, rules, and customs of reference groups that are applicable to a given position,
since all such rules and customs are role expectations associated
with this position. For can-expectations, which cannot be ascertained by this method, we can perhaps make use of the social psychologist's trick of "placing" a person by inferring his main social
positions from his appearance, language, and demeanor. This trick
can be reversed. Random groups of people[43] might be asked what
appearance and demeanor they think is expected of the incumbent
of a given position. Such replicable "experiments in definition"[44]
would give us guidelines at least for those can-expectations which
are not laid down in any law or statute and yet shape so much of the
behavior of *homo sociologicus*. Although it would be dangerous to
rely entirely on experiments in definition, they promise a welcome
addition to our ways of ascertaining must- and shall-expectations.

In these technical remarks, we are thinking of role descriptions
only as elements in a larger analysis, as data to be used in dealing
with specific problems. But such descriptions themselves may fur-
nish telling insights; indeed, literary descriptions of particular roles
historically preceded not only their strict definition, but the very
concept of role. Even in the sociological literature there are many
informative (if methodologically uncertain) descriptions of particular roles. Margaret Mead has investigated the specific features of
sex roles (23); S. N. Eisenstadt has done the same for age roles (11).
A small library might be filled with sociologists' descriptions of
occupational roles: railwayman and manager, druggist and boxer,

[43] The word "random" requires two qualifications here. First, it would not be
advisable to ask members of reference groups about positions determined by their
group, because that would make it difficult to distinguish between institutionalized
expectations and personal opinions. Second, it is necessary to choose respondents with
some knowledge of the positions in question; unskilled workers will be hard put to
pronounce on the position of accountant. Given these requirements, it makes good
sense (and methodologically it seems unobjectionable) to choose students or even
sociologists as respondents.

[44] The notion of experiments in definition and their application in social psychology is due to P. R. Hofstätter (14: 35ff) (15).

salesgirl and unskilled worker. Many studies of the characteristic behavior of certain social strata or classes (e.g. 2), as well as most works on the problematic subject of national character (e.g. 17), are essentially descriptions of roles. In all these cases, the comparative description of roles across historical and geographical boundaries has proved very fruitful.

A concern with particular roles leads to a concern with specific problems of sociological analysis, since it involves the confrontation of role expectations with actual behavior. We have already noted two aspects of this confrontation: the difference between roles and the actual behavior of their incumbents; and the difference between the norms of reference groups, insofar as these define role expectations, and their members' opinions of these norms. In both cases the role concept yields insights into the regularities of social change. Consider, for example, the role of Assistant in German universities, which is defined strictly in terms of learning and research; if in fact a majority of Assistants have teaching and administrative duties, it may be presumed that a change of role definitions is imminent. The extent of agreement between roles and actual behavior, between norms and opinions, is an index of social stability; disagreement indicates the presence of conflict, and thus the possibility and the likely direction of change.

The study of intra-role conflict is particularly important for the investigation of social structure. Thus Joseph Ben-David (4) has examined the role of the physician in bureaucratized medicine, who is expected to do his best by his patients while at the same time complying with administrative obligations that may run counter to his patients' interests. Such conflicts are usual in professional positions today; the so-called liberal professions are a thing of the past. Since the conflicting expectations of the two reference groups in this situation—clients or patients, and superordinate agencies— cannot both be met, some change in the social structure is imperative. So long as no such change occurs, the professional man must either break the law or act in a manner quite unintended by the reference groups (for example, a doctor may neglect his patients, whose sanctions are less severe than those of government agencies or insurance companies). Many problems of social behavior can be explained in terms of a conflict of expectations within roles.

The study of conflicts *within* roles became possible only with the concept of role segments; before that, however, there was some study of conflicts *between* roles, i.e., of the problems that arose when a person was obliged to play two or more roles with contradictory expectations. Some such inter-role conflicts are created and resolved by people's arbitrary choices; others, of far greater structural importance, are built into the process of position allocation. The man who cannot reconcile his simultaneous membership in two hostile political parties can leave one of them; but the member of parliament who must function as a businessman as well, or the worker's son who as a lawyer must comply with the expectations of his new and higher social level, finds himself in a conflict that he cannot escape by sheer choice. The familiar problem of the reduced significance of the family in industrial society has been successfully tackled with the help of these concepts. Neil Smelser, in his study of the Lancashire cotton industry during industrialization (41), has shown how the shift of production from the home to the factory led to a separation of familial and occupational roles and ultimately to a conflict between them. Whereas formerly a father combined his work and the education of his children, a father working in a factory had to separate the two functions and reduce the time and energy spent on one of them. The conflict between occupational and familial roles, and its gradual resolution by the reduction of the expectations associated with familial positions, can be documented in historical detail, and accordingly makes a good paradigm for many other processes of the social division of labor.

The role concept is clearly useful in analyzing how a single individual is affected by the conflict of expectations within and between his roles; but its usefulness does not stop there. Consider, for example, the problem of industrial conflict. Why is there a conflict between employers and workers? Is it because there is some inherent hostility between these groups? Are workers and employers, as people, irreconcilable foes? Obviously, such an assumption makes little sense; and yet it is at least implicit in many discussions of the

subject. With the categories developed here we can clarify the problem. Workers and employers are the incumbents of two types of
roles which are defined, among other things, by contradictory role
expectations. The conflict between the two role types is structural,
i.e., essentially independent of the feelings and views of the role
players themselves; it exists only insofar as Messrs. A, B, C are incumbents of the position "employer" and Messrs. X, Y, Z incumbents of the position "worker." In other positions—for example, as
members of a soccer club—A, B, C and X, Y, Z may be good friends.
All sociological statements about their relationship leave them unaffected as human beings; they are strictly statements about people
as incumbents of positions and players of roles.[45]

The example of industrial conflict is but one of many. There certainly are sociological problems that can be solved without direct
reference to social roles as there are sociological publications in
which the word "role" neither occurs nor needs to occur.[46] But even
such works, insofar as they are sociological, are nowhere concerned

[45] This approach to the explanation of industrial and political conflicts is elaborated in my book *Class and Class Conflict* (8). In outlining the empirical applications
of the category of role, I have deliberately given precedence here to problems of social
conflict. Structural-functional theorists, by contrast, tend to relate the elementary
categories of position and role to the so-called integration theory of society, a demonstrably one-sided analytical position. According to the integration theory, units of
social structure may be understood as systems; all the elements of a system contribute
to its functioning in a definable manner, and any element that does not so contribute
is eliminated from the analysis as "dysfunctional." Sensible as this approach may be
in certain cases, it would be wrong to generalize it and misleading to define role and
position in this restricted manner. We have defined roles as complexes of behavior
expectations adhering to social positions. This does not imply an exclusive focus on
behavior patterns that contribute to the functioning of an existing system. Behavior
that the integration theory would consider "dysfunctional" is equally subject to
norms, i.e., to being crystallized into role expectations. Thus even if the functioning
of the existing "system" is jeopardized by labor's wholesale rejection of the distribu-
tion of power in industry, there is every reason to regard labor's attitude as a behavior expectation associated with the position "worker."

[46] Analogies to natural science are objectionable to many social scientists, but one
seems worth proposing here. Even in physics by no means all problems directly involve the atom. Entire branches of physics—e.g., classical mechanics—have been developed without a single reference to atoms. Nevertheless it would be correct to describe the atom as a fundamental element of the physical sciences. Possibly role
sociology, i.e., the scientific concern with roles as such, will one day be a special field
like nuclear physics; such a development would not affect the fundamental character
of the role concept.

with the full human being, his feelings and desires, his idiosyncra-
sies and peculiarities. The assumptions and theories of sociology
refer not to man but to *homo sociologicus,* man in the alienated
aspect of an incumbent of positions and a player of roles. It is not
Schmidt the man but Schmidt the grammar school teacher who has
a relatively low income despite high social prestige; not Schmidt
the man but Schmidt the party official who asks questions from the
floor at meetings of the opposition party; not Schmidt the man but
Schmidt the driver who defends himself before the traffic judge
against the charge of speeding; not Schmidt the man but Schmidt
the husband and father who takes out an expensive life insurance
policy as protection for his family. And Schmidt the man? What
does he do? What can he do without being robbed of his individuality and converted into an incumbent of positions and a player of
roles? Does the man Schmidt begin where his roles end? Does he
live in his roles? Or is his a world in which roles and positions exist as little as neutrons and protons in the world of the housewife
who sets the table for dinner? This is the insistent paradox of *homo
sociologicus.* Our discussion of it will take us next to the region
where sociology and philosophy meet.

IX

"The inhabitant of a country," Robert Musil remarks, "has at
least nine characters: an occupational character, a national character, a civic character, a class character, a geographical character, a
sex character, a conscious character, and an unconscious character,
and perhaps a private character as well. He combines them all in
himself, but they dissolve him, and he is really nothing but a small
channel washed out by these trickling streams, which they flow into
and leave again to join other little streams and fill another channel. This is why every inhabitant of the earth has a tenth character as well, which is nothing more nor less than the passive fantasy
of unfilled spaces. It permits man everything except one thing: to
take seriously what his nine or more other characters do and what
happens to them. In other words, then, it forbids him precisely that

which would fulfill him." (26: 35.) Like the village chemist who outdid the BBC Meteorological Service with his "forecasts," the poet here anticipates the sociologist's insight into his subject matter. Musil does even more. His observation, which is equally remarkable for the richness of its substance and the irony of its form, establishes for the sociologist not merely the subject of his science, but also the limits of his method. Musil sees the paradox of the two human beings, and solves it in the irony of his reflection.

The inhabitant of a country is man in relation to society; he is not simply man, but man in a "country," living along with others within certain political boundaries on which he depends. As such, he has a number of characters, masks, personas, roles. Among these are his occupational, national, civic, class, regional, and sex characters; Musil might have added age, family, and others. Moreover, the inhabitant of a country is not merely *homo sociologicus*, but also psychological man; there are two souls in his breast, one his conscious Ego, the other his unconscious Id, and both are colors in the spectrum on which his figure oscillates. His characters, which are yet not his, leave him a small range of freedom, which, if he has the desire and ability, he may perhaps use for matters that are his and his alone. This private character stands alongside the other characters. Man "has" these characters, they are thoroughly his, and yet he has not made them. They have their reality outside him, and by taking them on he loses himself. They dissolve him. What remains is man as a "small channel washed out by these trickling streams," a player of roles that are no more of his devising than the laws of the country he lives in. His roles are conferred on him, and he is shaped by them; but when he dies, the impersonal force of society takes his roles away and confers them on somebody else in new combinations. From the unique, man has turned into the exemplar, from the individual into the member, from a free and autonomous creature into the sum of his alien characters.

But man, this particular human being Hans Schmidt whom we encounter at a party, is not merely the sum of his characters. We sense and know that there is something else about him, that he is not merely the inhabitant of a country but an inhabitant of the

earth, and as such free of all ties to society. His tenth character is
more than a mere supplement to the other nine; it rules an entire
world in which it tolerates no other characters beside itself; it en-
compasses all other characters and thus makes them disappear. Man
the inhabitant of a country is merely an object of ironical protest
for man the inhabitant of the earth. The claim to exclusiveness on
the part of the inhabitant of a country is nothing but a distant piece
of presumptuousness for the inhabitant of the earth, to which he
listens and about which he smiles without its ever penetrating the
spaces of his imagination. His tenth character dies with the inhabitant of the earth; it is entirely his and is administered by him alone.

Musil's ironic withdrawal to "the passive fantasy of unfilled
spaces" may not be the most satisfactory response to the paradox
of the two human beings; but his words make that paradox dra-
matically clear. However we turn and twist *homo sociologicus*, he
will never be the particular person who is our friend, colleague,
father, or brother. *Homo sociologicus* can neither love nor hate,
laugh nor cry. He remains a pale, incomplete, strange, artificial
man. Yet he is more than the showpiece of an exhibit. He provides
the standard by which our world—and indeed our friend, our colleague, our father, our brother—becomes comprehensible for us.
The world of *homo sociologicus* may not be the world of our experience, but the two are strikingly similar. If we identify with
homo sociologicus and his predetermined ways, our "tenth character" rises in protest; but we are nonetheless constrained to follow
his paths as they appear on the maps of sociology.

Two intentions were the godparents of sociology. The new discipline was supposed to make the fact of society accessible to rational
understanding by means of testable assumptions and theories, and
to help the individual toward freedom and self-fulfillment.[47] To-

[47] It seems to me that the origins of sociology may be traced to four social and intellectual constellations, each containing both moral and scientific impulses (though
in different mixtures). (1) Scotland in the late eighteenth century (after Hume), when
men like Adam Smith and Adam Ferguson, Sir John Sinclair and John Millar, were
concerned with understanding the breaking up of feudal society and the incipient
problem of industrialization. (2) France in the early nineteenth century, when men
like Saint-Simon and Comte were concerned with mastering the meaning of the
French Revolution. (3) Germany in the 1830's and 1840's (after Hegel), when David

day, Alfred Weber says what many feel when he mourns the "abundance of sociologies" which "no longer have as their focus man and his destiny as a whole," and maintains that "sociology is concerned with the structure and dynamics of human existence" (43: 13, 12). But Weber's formulation is not altogether fortunate, for it conceals a fundamental objection behind the appearance of a straightforward definition of the subject matter of sociology. According to Weber, whereas sociology after some decades of rapid development has come considerably closer to a rational understanding of the fact of society, the autonomous human being and his freedom have been lost sight of in the process. By constructing *homo sociologicus*, sociologists have let Herr Schmidt, with his unique individuality and his personal claim to respect and freedom, slip through their fingers. Sociology has paid for the exactness of its propositions with the humanity of its intentions, and has become a thoroughly inhuman, amoral science.

Alfred Weber and the many who share this view are mistaken in one important respect. It was no accident that in the course of time sociology lost sight of people as human beings; rather, this development was inevitable from the moment that sociology emerged as a science. The two intentions with which sociology began are incompatible.[48] As long as sociologists interpret their task in moral terms, they must renounce the analysis of social reality; as soon as they strive for scientific insight, they must forgo their moral concern with the individual and his liberty. What makes the paradox of moral and alienated man so urgent is not that sociology has strayed from its proper task, but that it has become a true science. The former process would be reversible, but the latter leads to an inescap-

---

Friedrich Strauss, Ludwig Feuerbach, Bruno and Edgar Bauer, Arnold Ruge, Moses Hess, Friedrich Engels, and Karl Marx took two steps simultaneously: from criticizing religion to criticizing society, and from theory to practice. (4) England in the late 1880's (1889 saw the publication of the first *Fabian Essays* and the organization of the great trade unions of the unskilled), when George Bernard Shaw, Beatrice and Sidney Webb, Charles Booth, and other social politicians perceived that they could realize their goals only if they thoroughly understood the workings of society. It is with this background in mind that I speak of the two intentions of sociology.

[48] Max Weber's notion of "value-free social science" is relevant here. See *Essays in the Theory of Society*, 1–18, 256–278, and section X below.

able question. Is man a social being whose behavior, being predetermined, is calculable and controllable? Or is he an autonomous
individual, with some irreducible measure of freedom to act as he
chooses?

So far we have referred to the paradox of the two human beings
as if it were beyond theoretical or practical resolution. At this
point, we shall have to see whether this is really so. Is there a necessary contradiction between the moral image of man as an integral,
unique, and free creature and his scientific image as a differentiated, exemplary aggregate of predetermined roles? Must we assume
that man is either one or the other, so that either our moral experience or our scientific reconstruction is wrong? At least one aspect
of this question, that of the free or conditioned character of human
action, has been dealt with extensively by Kant in his third antinomy of pure reason; and since Kant was concerned with the same
paradox that concerns us, we may do well to follow his argument.
The paradox has two motifs or aspects, which we have made no
effort to connect. One is that the man of our experience is free,
whereas *homo sociologicus* is determined; the other is that the inhabitant of the earth is an undivided whole, whereas the inhabitant of a country appears to us as a mere sum, or set, of impersonal
elements. Kant's discussion can be applied to both aspects.

In the language of Kant, *homo sociologicus* is man under the
spell of natural "laws";[49] his every move is merely a link in a chain
of recognizable relations. The integral individual, by contrast, cannot be linked to such a chain; he is free. Each of these two versions
of man can be justified by a logically conclusive argument; they are
thesis and antithesis of an argument that defies immanent resolution:

> Thus nature and transcendental freedom differ in the same
> way as lawfulness and lawlessness. The former may burden our

---

[49] Kant himself occasionally, and especially in his *Anthropology*, touches on the
borders of social science, but essentially "lawfulness" and "lawfulness according to
the laws of nature" are the same to him. Today the notion of "natural laws" appears
dubious to natural scientists and even more dubious to social scientists. It suggests the
idea of an immanent necessity behind scientific theories, which (as we know thanks
in large part to Kant) remain always hypothetical.

reason with the difficulty of seeking the origin of events ever higher in the chain of causation, because all causality is determined; but it offers as a reward the all-pervading unity of experience in accordance with laws. By contrast, the deceptive glitter of freedom[50] promises calm to the searching mind in the chain of causation by leading it to an uncaused first cause that acts of itself; but this first cause, being blind, shrugs off the guiding light of rules, by which alone a completely coherent experience is possible. (18: 463.)

According to Kant, each of the two—nature and freedom, *homo sociologicus* and the integral human being—has its charms and deficiencies. The thesis of freedom may be "dogmatic" and "speculative," but it is no less popular for these drawbacks, especially since it accords with our "practical interest." In the antithesis of lawfulness "moral ideals and principles lose all validity" (18: 474), but by way of compensation we are given a reliable and orderly "empirical" means of comprehending the world. Both sides are given to a certain "lack of modesty" (18: 477). The sociologist describes man as an aggregate of roles, and unthinkingly goes on to claim that he has discovered the nature of man. His opponent, in the name of the integral human being, disputes the sociologist's very right to dissect man into his components and reconstruct him scientifically.

If and only if we assume—so Kant goes on to argue—that outside our experience but accessible to it there is a being in itself, a *Ding an sich*, the contradiction between the two theses is indeed an unresolvable antinomy. But there is no evidence to support such an assumption. Rather, the transcendental critique shows that thesis and antithesis, inhabitant of the earth and inhabitant of a country, do not contradict each other but are simply different ways of comprehending the same subject, ways that derive from different sources of knowledge. Kant makes this point in a metaphor so strik-

---

50 The quotation is taken from Kant's argument for the antithesis ("There is no freedom, but everything in the world happens merely by the laws of nature"), and therefore does not do justice to the argument for the thesis of freedom. This context explains the expression "deceptive glitter of freedom."

ingly like Musil's observation (not to mention our stage metaphors)
that one is almost tempted to wonder whether Musil has translated
Kant into his freer language:

> But every efficient cause must have a *character*, i.e., a law gov-
> erning its causality, without which it would not be a cause at all.
> And so we should find in a subject of the world of the senses first
> of all an *empirical character*, by which its actions, as phenomena,
> are connected with other phenomena by permanent laws of na-
> ture in such a way that these actions can be derived from the
> other phenomena, so that the two together constitute a single
> row of the order of nature. Second, we should have to allow it
> an *intelligible character*, by which it is the cause of those actions
> as phenomena, but which is not itself in any way accessible to the
> senses, not a phenomenon. One might call the first the character
> of the thing as a phenomenon, the second the character of the
> thing in itself. (18: 527–28.)

Musil dissolves Kant's empirical character into a series of characters; but Kant's intelligible character is precisely Musil's "tenth
character," a unit of an utterly different kind from the others. As
a phenomenon, i.e., in his observable behavior, man is a role-playing, determinate creature. But he has in addition a character of
freedom and integrity, which is completely unaffected by his phe-
nomenal character and its laws. "Thus freedom and nature, each
in its complete meaning, would in the same actions, depending on
whether one considers their intelligible or their sensible cause, be
encountered simultaneously and without any contradiction." (18:
529.)

Kant states explicitly that man is one of the phenomena of the
world of the senses to which these considerations apply; from the
discussion of this "example" he derives his distinction between
understanding (*Verstand*) and reason (*Vernunft*) (18: 533). Every
man has an empirical character, and this character is strictly determined; in studying it, "we are simply observing [man], and in the
manner of anthropology seeking to explore the motive cause of his
actions physiologically" (18: 536). In addition, and at the same

time, every man has an intelligible character, a practical reason that makes him a free and moral being. The antinomy of human knowledge is thus revealed as merely apparent; there is no plausible reason to reject Kant's conclusion that the two characters "may exist independently of each other and undisturbed by each other" (18: 541). Although the free, integral individual is not accessible to empirical research and cannot be, we know about him in ourselves and in others. And although the constructed, conditioned exemplar is based on the systematic study of phenomena, all the study in the world cannot make it more than a construction of the mind. The paradox of the two human beings, if it exists at all, is different in kind from the paradox of the two tables. Whereas the latter opposes two genuinely contradictory ways of seeing the same phenomena, the former is dispelled by a critical review of its epistemological basis. The two shapes of the table are competing theories in the same sphere of knowledge; the two characters of man are an expression of essentially different possibilities of knowledge.

Although Kant's arguments fully apply to our context, the paradox of the two human beings is by no means a mirage. We never claimed that it was identical with the paradox of the two tables; instead we have described it from the outset as more urgent, more inescapable, more important to come to terms with, than the paradox of the tables. The difference in urgency can now be made explicit. If we speak of the physicist's table and the table of our experience, we assert a paradox consisting of the statements "This table is smooth and solid" and "This table is (not smooth and solid, but) a beehive of nuclear particles." But the paradox of the two human beings involves more than the apparent difference between the statements "Man is indivisible and free" and "Man is an aggregate of roles and conditioned." With respect to our knowledge of man these two statements are not even contradictory. They become contradictory only when we translate them from the transcendental into the empirical sphere, and relate them to the practical problems of ethics. Here the conditioned man poses a moral problem as the nuclear table does not and cannot. Whenever we deal with human beings, we must consider not only pure knowledge but the

practical realm of morality; and in this realm our paradox changes
from a question of knowledge that can be examined (or evaded)
into a problem that must be faced before any meaningful progress
can be made. We do not have to decide whether man is an "inhabitant of a country" or an "inhabitant of the earth." We do have to
decide whether sociology, by transforming man into *homo sociologicus,* has gone against its original intentions and become a pro-
moter, or at least an unprotecting supporter, of unfreedom and
inhumanity.

X

Historians were the first social scientists to see the conflict between integral man and his sociological shadow, and to resolve it,
precariously, for their own discipline. At least since history's claim
to scientific status was asserted in the nineteenth century, it has
been debated whether a systematic concern with history can stop
at science, or whether it must not always include a measure of art.[51]
Not all historians have been advocates of an artistically inspired
historiography; Clio is one of many victims of the nineteenth century. But every historian worth the name knows that even the best
scientific theories of economics, psychology, and sociology can hardly help him re-create the past. As soon as he gets beyond testing abstract assumptions against specific situations, as soon as he tries to
catch a single historical situation in its human richness and tragic
depth, the theories of science desert him, leaving him with integral
man and the passive fantasy of unfilled spaces. The historian cannot reconstruct Herr Schmidt from his roles. If historiography were
merely a testing ground for the more rigorous social sciences, there
would be no need to worry about it. But it is clearly more than a
testing ground. The historian's purposes, artistic and pragmatic
alike, demand more immediate access to the actors of past dramas
than sociology can offer.

The historian's problem is not a problem of scientific knowledge.

---

[51] Fritz Stern's anthology *The Varieties of History* (42) follows this discussion
through two centuries; the following remarks are stimulated by this volume.

Rather, it stems from the fact that once science deals with man, the logical separation between the man of science and the man of our everyday experience becomes insignificant for all practical purposes. With respect to our actions, the "inhabitant of the earth" and the "inhabitant of a country" are not two spheres that exist side by side wihout ever disturbing each other. Musil is quite right in saying that the inhabitant of the earth fails to take seriously the very things that would fulfill him. What is more, he opposes the inhabitant of a country on principle for trying to fill his unfilled spaces with alien laws. Insofar as *homo sociologicus* is more than the private toy of hermits pursuing their exercises of contemplation on distant mountains, he becomes a challenge to moral man and his goals.

The paradox that Kant's transcendental critique cannot resolve arises from the moral effect of the notion of *homo sociologicus* in a society that is only too ready to replace its common sense by scientific theories.[52] Already our courts of law are finding it difficult to reconcile the expert opinions of social scientists with the guilt of the accused. For the sociologically schooled journalist and his readers, even the most inhuman political movement becomes a "necessary" consequence of identifiable causes and conditions. We may not be far from the point at which *homo sociologicus*, man without individuality or moral responsibility, replaces the completely autonomous integral individual as the basis of men's self-perception and thus of their actions. It is this practical competition between *homo sociologicus* and the human being of our experience that has produced our dilemma. Because *homo sociologicus* as a product of science has the advantage in our century, it is urgent that some effort be made to resolve this paradox, or at least to clarify it.

[52] The problem in question here was not unfamiliar to Kant; but its solution in the *Critique of Practical Reason* misses the core of the dilemma. What Kant—for good reason—treats as an intellectual problem is today above all a social problem. To put this another way, the dilemma of the two human beings comes neither from the incompatibility of statements about the two nor from a doubt in principle about which of the two should serve as the practical basis of morals. Rather, it comes from the social influence of sociology and the spreading of sociological assumptions in hypostatized form, which logical criticism has proved powerless to stop.

We may note, not without irony, that the fault of sociology in creating this dilemma is not the fault of sociologists. The old saw *tout comprendre c'est tout pardonner* holds here, as it does for any practical application of science. As it happens, it now seems clear that sociology, being concerned solely with the empirical character of man, had to enter a sphere in which, as Kant says, "moral ideals and principles lose all validity"; while at the same time, owing to its concern with man and the necessity of making its findings public and teaching them in the university, it had to become a moral force in society. In terms of sociology's two original intentions, the sociologist has an unresolvable role conflict. On the one hand, he is expected to proceed scientifically, and thus, if necessary for analytic purposes, to deal with man as *homo sociologicus*; on the other hand, he is expected to help liberate man from his subservience to external purposes, and thus to deal with Herr Schmidt as an autonomous, free individual. Here, however, an element of choice and of possible guilt in sociologists' behavior becomes apparent after all. Like the doctor who decides to neglect his patients rather than lose favor with officials in the public health insurance organization, sociologists have been too ready to give up their moral mandate for the cool precision of scientific method. This choice brings few recriminations. Generally speaking, people have as little hold over the sociologists who investigate them as patients have over their doctors,[53] whereas bureaucratized organizations and the community of scholars are always ready to subject their aberrant members to the sanction of expulsion. Nevertheless the choice is a bad one, and its consequences in the large seem likely to be incomparably more severe (if they are not already) than the consequences of the alternative decision.

It is ironic, almost tragic, that the man who made sociology's decision in favor of science, and thus against its moral mandate, was perhaps more aware than any other sociologist of the paradox of

---

[53] This assertion requires two qualifications. On the one hand, there is at least a remote chance (increasingly exploited in the United States) for patients to bring suit against physicians for malpractice. On the other hand, the hypostatized society of the sociologist—the total state—constitutes an indirect sanction whose severity is beyond doubt.

the two human beings. Nevertheless, there can be little doubt that Max Weber's rigid separation of science and value judgments, his insistence on a value-free social science, has led to the abandonment of sociology's moral intention. Without doubt, this was not Weber's purpose. In demanding that value judgments and moral impulses be punctiliously kept separate from scientific concerns, he sought to restore both science and values to their proper dignity. His great error lay in his failure to see that social science and its findings themselves constitute a great moral force, which, if it is not deliberately harnessed, works so strongly against liberty and individuality that a morality independent of science cannot withstand it. What Weber's powerful if explosive personality could unite—the rigor of value-free science and the passion of a moral position—his successors could not. A value-free sociology became established, but the concern with man's freedom and autonomy disappeared.[54]

Weber's error is not in the logic of his distinction, which is unassailable. He is right to warn against confusing values and scientific insights; indeed, his distinction between the two is a legitimate application of Kant's distinction between the empirical and the intelligible character. Weber's error is one of emphasis. This, too, is historically and biographically understandable. The discussions in the Verein für Sozialpolitik left him no choice but to emphasize in his arguments the points at which mixing science and value judgments would lead to harmful consequences for both.[55] But today Weber's opponents in these discussions are forgotten, whereas his arguments (backed by his prestige) are very much alive, with the result that they are often taken out of context and through no fault of Weber's do more harm than good. Many sociologists are still hardly aware of the hypothetical character of their artificial

[54] For a further discussion of Weber's position, see my essay, "Values and Social Science" in *Essays in the Theory of Society*.

[55] If there is any fault to be found here, it is first of all in the Value Dispute itself, which continues to cast its shadow over German social science. The aspect of the Dispute that has caused the most trouble is the unlikely combination of political conservatism and value-laden science in the thought of Weber's opponents, and political criticism and value-free science in Weber's own thought. Many of the effects of Weber's thesis can be better understood in the light of this "false" confrontation.

man. When they speak of the human personality as an aggregate of roles, they ignore man's "tenth character," his intelligible, moral character, without which he becomes a horrible phantom of the totalitarian imagination. If even sociologists exhibit confusion on this point, one can hardly blame their students and others for following them. And it is only a step from seeing man as a mere role player to the alienated world of "1984," where all loving and hating, all dreaming and acting, all individuality beyond the grasp of roles, becomes a crime against society—society in this sense being sociology hypostatized.

Since Weber's time, the pragmatic problem of the two human beings has gained rather than lost in urgency, and the time has accordingly come for us to revise our position toward it. In doing so, to repeat, we are not challenging the logical validity of the distinction between science and value judgments. Nobody wants an ideologized science, a science that consciously or unconsciously offers scientific theories as moral precepts or vice versa. Here, Weber is as far from being superseded as Karl Mannheim, Theodor Geiger, and other critics of ideology. But to require the sociologist to select projects that seem likely to benefit the cause of the individual and his liberty is not to reestablish ideology. The sociologist does not endanger the purity of his scientific activity by preferring to work with testable theories that recognize the individual's rights and the richness of his life. It is methodologically quite above suspicion for a social scientist to keep an eye out for ways of making his own findings further individual freedom and self-fulfillment.

Behind these specific demands there is something else, something even more important. No amount of critical analysis can finally resolve the dilemma of the two human beings; we can at best hope to master it satisfactorily in our actions. Both *homo sociologicus* and the free individual are part of our world and the way we interpret that world. It follows that the sociologist must first of all recognize the dilemma and keep its urgency in mind. Anyone who cannot bear the melancholy insufficiency of a sociological science of man should renounce the discipline, for a dogmatic sociology is worse than no sociology at all. The sociologist has every reason to envy historians their opportunity to merge the person Hans Schmidt and his role-playing shadow in a single work—their opportunity, that is, to combine science and art. He himself does not have this opportunity. It is the more difficult for him to keep in mind the dilemma of the two human beings, and not to lose sight of the autonomous individual in his concern with *homo sociologicus*. In sociological investigations Herr Schmidt the person has no place, yet he must never be forgotten. Awareness of the autonomous individual and his claim to liberty must inform every sentence the sociologist speaks and writes; society must constantly be present to him not only as a fact, but as a vexation; the moral insufficiency of his discipline must always appear as a passionate undertone in his work. Only by replacing the unintended practical effects of a seemingly pure sociological science with effects that are consciously intended to be advantageous to the individual and his freedom can we hope to translate the dilemma of the two human beings into fruitful action.

The sociologist as such is not, and should not be, a politician. But even worse is the sociologist who sees the career of a scientist as requiring him to renounce all critical concern with his own actions and his society. The abstention of the non-voter always favors the stronger party; and in practical matters in general, no abstention is without consequences. It is but a weak consolation for the sociologist, therefore, that Kant's transcendental critique finds *homo sociologicus* compatible with the free individual. The practical dilemma remains. Only if the sociologist selects his research projects with an eye to what may help liberate the individual from the vexations of society, if he formulates his hypotheses with a view to extending men's range of free choice, if he does not shy away from supporting political changes designed to increase individual freedom, and if he never forgets the superior rights of Herr Schmidt the person over his role-playing shadow—only then can he hope to use the insights of sociology to protect man the inhabitant of the earth from the boundless demands of man the inhabitant of a country. Only then can the sociologist cease being a brake and become a motor of a society of free men, a society whose vexatiousness, along with the all too passive fantasy of unfilled spaces, is swallowed up in the active reality of freely filled time.

2

Sociology and Human Nature
A Postscript to Homo Sociologicus

That sociology is a science of man is one of those dangerously imprecise formulations that stand in the way of scientific understanding, and not for the layman alone. Of course, a theory of social classes, an analysis of the social structure of a city or an office, an investigation of authority in the family, and an explanation of political revolution are all concerned with things human. But so are the theories of human biology and psychology, of economics and anthropology. And so also, after all, are historiography and pedagogy, jurisprudence and philology, medicine and art history; yet to describe these last as sciences of man would be to say nothing significant about them.

Nor would it be correct to say that each of these disciplines (along with others not mentioned) deals with but one aspect of the total problem of man, so that man is, as it were, the synthetic subject matter of them all. Indeed, the error in speaking of sciences of man (and, for that matter, of natural sciences) lies precisely in the implication that scientific disciplines can be defined in terms of their so-called subject matter. It would be very daring even to assume that our encyclopedia of scientific subjects and disciplines represents in any meaningful way the articulation of the world. It seems proper, therefore, to acknowledge that the range of problems dealt with under the name of a given scientific discipline is determined by basically arbitrary traditions, and is therefore potentially subject at any time to expansion or contraction. Thus it can happen that matters which a decade ago were regarded by men in a given discipline as a suitable subject of research are today indignantly rejected by those in the same discipline.[1] Probably academic recognition of a new discipline always betokens the fragmentation or redefinition of these arbitrary traditions.

Now it would obviously be an exaggeration to claim that sociology has attained as firm a consensus as older disciplines on the matter of what problems to investigate and how to approach them. What sociologists call sociology is still a mixed bag of many different problems, modes of statement, and claims to knowledge—to say nothing of what non-sociologists hold to be sociology. Anyone who knows the tendency among American sociologists to define the mandate of their discipline prematurely on the basis of a consensus that at times seems rather forced, will not regret the presence in Europe of a lively debate on this subject; here as elsewhere, conflict generates progress. In recent years, however, there has unmistakably been increasing agreement among European sociologists about the place of human behavior in what are generally described as sociological theories. One symptom of this agreement is the increasing use of a certain set of categories, notably position, role, role expectation, and sanction.

It is widely agreed, and attested to by the poetry of all ages, that people invariably perceive each other as the possessors of certain attributes or the incumbents of certain *positions*: father and son, colleague and colleague, superior and subordinate, German and Frenchman, etc. Every such social position—and there must always be more than one, because society is not conceivable without a degree of internal differentiation[2]—defines a field of social relations. In saying "teacher," we are saying (not of course analytically, but

[1] A proof and at the same time a further illustration of this thesis may be found in the fact that definitions of disciplines with identical names—among them sociology, psychology, and social policy—vary considerably from country to country.

[2] Aristotle's statement "When all are equal, there can be no state" (45: 1261a) may also be correctly interpreted to mean that at least some division of labor and social stratification, or differentiation of kind and of rank, is always implied when we speak of society. To the sociologists, in contrast to Aristotle, it is not people who are distinguished by kind and rank, but their social positions.

synthetically) "teacher-pupil," "teacher-teacher," "teacher–school administration," "teacher-parents"—i.e., we are establishing a field of positions around the central position in question. Theoretically, every society may be represented as a huge, multidimensional structure of such relations.[3] This concept of society is the basis of recent attempts to simulate social processes with the help of electronic computers.

What makes the structure of social positions come to life is role behavior. By virtue of being a certain someone, we do certain things; more precisely, our social position not merely places us into a field with other positions, but also gives other people more or less specific *expectations* of us. For every position, then, there is a *social role,* a set of modes of behavior that is ascribed to the incumbent. American sociologists like to describe roles as the "dynamic aspect of positions"; it would probably be better to describe them as what lends substance to the empty form of social positions.

A great many conceptual and theoretical questions (which will not be considered here) arise from this approach.[4] But for our argument it is important to remember that even if we can strive for social positions and roles, that is, even if they are attainable by our efforts, they are of course not subject to our defining. The field of relations in which a position places us, and the set of expectations associated with it, are binding on us as soon as we become the incumbent of that position and the player of the associated role. The system of social *sanctions,* i.e., of rewards for conforming and punishments for deviant behavior, guarantees that we will not evade this binding character of roles.

With the assistance of these few categories (explained here very inadequately), we may formulate the proposition that implicitly or explicitly underlies all research and theoretical work in modern sociology: *Man behaves in accordance with his roles.* Thus man basically figures in sociological analyses only to the extent that he com-

---

[3] What is meant by multidimensional is that Mr. X stands as "teacher" in one field, as "father" in a second, as "German" in a third, etc. A "society" is a highly complex structure consisting of all such position fields for all its members.

[4] Some of them have been discussed in the foregoing essay, "Homo Sociologicus."

plies with all the expectations associated with his social positions. This abstraction, the scientific unit of sociology, may be called *homo sociologicus.* In an angry and critical mood, one might say that sociology is the science, and thus the instrument, of conformism; to put the same point less angrily and more precisely, sociological theories equate the playing of social roles with the whole of human behavior.

To discuss the scientific implications of this statement would require little less than an encyclopedia of the social sciences. We would have to ask how the categories I have mentioned, "role" and "position," relate to the other basic categories of sociology, "norm" and "power." We would have to investigate the interaction of individual personality (in the sense of recent psychological theory) and social role. Finally, we would have to consider the great problems of role theory itself. For example, are there typical "role-sets" (Merton) that fall to individuals in given societies? What is the structural significance of the distinction between achieved and ascribed positions? How can incompatible role expectations or roles be reconciled? Under what conditions and in what ways do social roles change? With such questions, role theory soon blends into general sociology, a field whose every question has to do with the concept, empirical identification, and analysis of social roles, and with man as *homo sociologicus.*

II

That the category of role and especially the postulate of role-conforming behavior have significance beyond their sociological applications is clear even to sociologists (although it is probably no accident that European sociologists make more of this point than American sociologists). What this extra-sociological significance involves can hardly be illuminated more ironically than by comparing the opening sentences of two very different essays on this subject. Helmuth Plessner, in whose work it is hard to separate sociology from philosophy, writes: "In defining sociology as a science, it seems perfectly plausible at first to require that it be concerned exclusively with social phenomena that are strictly capable of being experienced, and that as an empirical discipline it detach itself once and for all from philosophical speculation." (59: 150.) In contrast, a critical representative of the empirical sociology Plessner is describing, Hans Paul Bahrdt, begins: "At first glance it seems almost a matter of course that sociology must have an 'image of man'; it even seems reasonable that sociology should have a special 'sociological image of man' determined by the peculiar nature of its subject and its secular role." (46: 1.) It is clear from their choice of words ("at first," "at first glance") that both Plessner and Bahrdt intend to reject the arguments they describe as "perfectly plausible" and "a matter of course"; but the conflict between the two positions as described is enough to indicate how far the significance of *homo sociologicus* transcends the borders of the discipline.

Clearly the assumption that all men behave in accordance with their roles at all times is demonstrably false. At one time or another, almost everyone violates the expectations associated with his positions. One might infer, therefore, that all sociological theories, insofar as they operate on this assumption, are bad theories; and in fact this point is occasionally made by laymen, and even scholars, who do not understand the logic of scientific discovery. Actually, misunderstandings of this kind cause little trouble. In economic theory the protracted argument over whether a *homo oeconomicus* who permanently weighs profits and losses is a realistic image of man's economic behavior has been decided: literal realism is quite unnecessary so long as the theories based on this model provide powerful explanations and useful predictions. Extreme advocates of the modern deductive-logic school of science—notably its founder, Karl Popper—at times go so far as to say that the less realistic the assumptions, the better the theory. What this statement means obviously depends on what we mean by a "good" theory, and thus by a "better" one. Since this question is important in our context, let us consider it in the light of an example.

It has been widely observed in German universities that students of working-class origin are the most inclined to join dueling fraternities. It has also been observed that upwardly mobile people are more inclined to vote for conservative political parties than people who have not risen above their parents' social position. How can we explain such observations? In both cases we encounter a version of role conflict, namely the conflict between what is expected of the people concerned as children of their parents and what is expected of them in their new positions, acquired by upward mobility. A young man's parents may vote for a radical party, but in his new.social stratum he votes conservative. Now the assumption that man behaves as *homo sociologicus* makes possible a general explanatory proposition: that a person in a situation of role conflict will always choose the role with which the stronger sanctions are associated. In our two cases, it seems clear that for the working-class student, and even more for the person whose career is well under way, the parents' sanctions are relatively mild compared with those of their new peers. This is why people go against their parents in these cases. It follows as a prediction that the working-class child who rises socially will in due course deny and betray his origins many times.

This is an example of a "good" sociological theory. It allows us to derive from a general statement definite, precise, and unrestricted predictions, and it has considerable explanatory power with respect, say, to the voting behavior of people who have risen socially from working-class origins. All this is true even though the role conformity assumed by the theory is obviously "unrealistic," in the sense that there are many people who do not behave in the manner postulated here. If we should now try to make our assumption "realistic," the entire theory would fall to pieces. The following statement would clearly be more "realistic": "In the face of role conflict, many people (perhaps 60 per cent) are inclined to prefer the role with which the stronger sanctions are associated; others (say 25 per cent) behave in accordance with moral principles without regard to social sanctions; and some (say 15 per cent) react to role conflicts with complete resignation or passivity."[5] Such a statement is all very well, but it can no longer be used to explain anything. To the extent that the assumptions underlying scientific

[5] The percentages in this statement are entirely fictitious.

theories become "realistic," they also become differentiated, restricted, ambiguous, unconducive to definite explanations or predictions. In this sense, then, the less realistic and more stylized, definite, and unambiguous the assumptions underlying a theory are,
the better the theory is.[6]

With this methodological excursus behind us, we can now turn
to the question of the meta-sociological significance of *homo sociologicus*, or sociology's image of man. If one assigns to sociology—as
by no means all sociologists do—the task of formulating precise
theories in the sense indicated above, and if one sees the construct
homo sociologicus in this context, then this construct in no way
implies an image of man. F. H. Tenbruck would then be quite
right in substance (though his formulation is a little unfortunate)
when he describes social role as "a construct by which, within the
limits indicated, we can calculate the behavior of man as a social
creature, without making any claim to describe this behavior as
it occurs in reality" (62: 29).[7]

Indeed, as a stylized and empirically almost arbitrary construct,
homo sociologicus explicitly renounces a sociological image of man:
it proclaims the intention of finding powerful explanatory theories
of social action rather than describing the nature of man accurately
and realistically. The reason why sociology in this sense has no image of man is not (as Plessner repeatedly seems to suggest) that sociology "renounces" certain questions and kinds of statements,[8]
but that scientific theories yield statements that are entirely different in range and purpose from statements about the nature of man.
To put the matter paradoxically, at the risk of being misunderstood: even if sociology asks questions about man, it is in substance

[6] It hardly need be mentioned that the point of view defended here is very rigorous; it implies, among other things, that even very precise probability statements cannot be accepted as theories. For the everyday requirements of science, this rigor would
undoubtedly have to be mitigated.

[7] The formulation is unfortunate because a mere "calculation" does not suffice to
justify a reliance on "unrealistic" assumptions.

[8] See, for example, 59: 150: "[Sociology's] renunciation of the questions of universal history and the psychological analysis of motives is offset by an anticipated gain
in insight into the internal mechanisms that condition the social life of men and thus
make their socialization possible."

concerned not with man but with ways of reducing man's actions to rational terms. Not only is sociology improperly defined as a science of man, but it is fundamentally indifferent to man as such, since it can reach much further with *homo sociologicus* than with statements that aim at an accurate description of man's nature.

III

This radical distinction between scientific sociology and philosophical anthropology is necessary if we are to avoid minimizing, by one facile formulation or another, the seriousness of the problem that concerns us here. For although the conclusion that sociology as a science neither has nor needs an image of man, and in particular that *homo sociologicus* cannot provide such an image, may be the last word on our problem in terms of the logic of science, we must remember that the logic of science is only one aspect of methodology. We must also deal with certain other aspects, aspects that are not logical but moral and even political. In recent discussions of sociology's image of man, there have been repeated references to the "reification" of *homo sociologicus* (although not always using this term, which is preeminently Tenbruck's). By reification is meant the reinterpretation or misinterpretation of a deliberately unrealistic assumption, made in the interests of good scientific theory, as a realistic description of the nature of man.[9] Of course, it is both easy and necessary to guard against this kind of reification of postulates. But first one should ask whether there might not be certain peculiarities of social science, and of sociology in particular, that at least encourage the reification of categories and postulates, and perhaps make it empirically almost unavoidable. In my opinion there are, and it is only from the perspective of these peculiarities that the real problem of a sociological image of man becomes apparent.

Earlier we observed that if sociology is defined as an empirical science, *homo sociologicus* has no implications for the nature of

---

[9] I confess to a certain amusement at Tenbruck's charging me, of all people, with reification; see section IV below.

man. As we have seen, however, this view of sociology is by no means generally accepted. Indeed, so many people see sociology's domain and methodology in so many different ways that logical arguments alone do not suffice to counter the tendency to reification. There are several kinds of sociologists who do not see sociology as an empirical science: those who, in pursuing Wilhelm Dilthey's tradition of irrationalism, deny in principle the possibility of rigorous theories in the so-called sciences of the mind (*Geisteswissenschaften*); those who, while they admit this possibility, nevertheless see the task of sociology as interpretative analysis on the model of history, that is, as striving for the highest possible degree of descriptive "realism"; and those who are indifferent to the distinction between testable and speculative statements, and thus between the statements of sociology and those of philosophical anthropology. To all such sociologists, the idea of inventing *homo sociologicus* as a deliberately "unrealistic" fiction for the sole purpose of formulating powerful explanatory theories must seem meaningless, or at least incomprehensible. Since they do not recognize the epistemological basis of the postulate of role-conforming behavior, *homo sociologicus* to them is not even an example of reification, but simply anthropological speculation masquerading as science. As long, then, as scientists of the mind and philosophical sociologists are as numerous as they are in European sociology (a situation, if I may say so without unduly confusing the issue, that is by no means to its detriment), the objective reification of sociological postulates will not be halted simply by repeating *ad nauseam* the claims of a nominalist epistemology and the associated logic of science.

A second reason for the inadequacy of the purely logical argument is even more significant, for it is inescapable. Science is not possible without publicity; the notion of a "secret science" contains a *contradictio in adiecto*.[10] Now in the traditional sciences (including economics) publicity means essentially professional pub-

---

[10] This statement, made dogmatically here, is by no means a matter of course—especially in the country that invented the absurdity of "inner freedom." On the contrary, it expresses a logic of scientific research that is specifically predicated on the fundamental uncertainty of human knowledge. See my essay "Uncertainty, Science, and Democracy" in *Essays in the Theory of Society*.

licity: i.e., discussion by a circle of people who agree on basic principles, or, more precisely, by a circle of people who have all accepted the second life of science and its moral conventions. But in the newer social sciences, as well as in psychology, the situation is different. Here publicity frequently means "general publicity"; publications in sociology, social psychology, and psychology are read by many people who have never seriously considered becoming scientists. It would be unrealistic for a social scientist to ignore this public effect of his research—an effect, by the way, that may be measured partly, though by no means solely, by the circulation figures of professional publications. The "general public" has no understanding at all of the subtle distinction between statements meant "realistically" and deliberately "unrealistic" postulates; indeed such postulates involve a fundamental deviation from the world of common sense which is at the very heart of the first contradiction between science and common sense.[11] Instead, the wider public sees *homo sociologicus* as the scientific truth about man.[12]

Nothing could demonstrate more clearly how misleading it is to speak of the "scientific orientation" of our world. Possibly the number of people who try to orient themselves by scientific theories or research findings is greater today than ever before; but an understanding of the peculiar nature of scientific statements is as rare today as it ever was. That science is knowledge based on logical supposition, that many scientific statements can by no means be taken literally, and above all that science does not impart certainty, is even today known at best to those who are personally engaged in the effort to catch the world of experience in the net of their theories. It follows that the public, which cannot and must not be denied access to scientific research, is bound to make the mistake of reifying *homo sociologicus* to some extent, and hence that the sociologist must address himself to this misunderstanding.

---

11 This statement is not intended to express a value judgment, and is certainly not meant as a depreciation of common sense.

12 Even the expression "scientific truth" can be defended only ironically. That science is capable of providing irrefutable truths is one of the serious errors of common sense.

It is an old question whether people may be held responsible for the unintended consequences of their actions. In terms of motivation, many a great teacher would have to be acquitted of the errors of his disciples, but in other cases things are not so clear. Who can say whether the Soviet Union is Marx's fault? Perhaps an attitude of legal positivism is best in such cases. From this point of view we may impute guilt by omission to the sociologist who, in full awareness of the damage done by his theories, washes his innocent hands in the pure logic of scientific discovery. To repeat, because the postulates of sociological analysis are likely (if not certain) to be misunderstood both inside and outside the discipline, the sociologist must leave the comfortable refuge of his logical righteousness and take a moral stand for or against the anthropological interpretations of his misunderstood theories.

Obviously the need for such a clarification does not in any way dictate its substance. To be sure, the sociologist's statement must specify that he never intended *homo sociologicus* as an image of man; but we have seen that this logical statement is not enough. What is needed next is itself anthropological and thus valuational, and—if one wants to call it that—moral. For the sociologist will have to state whether he accepts or rejects the anthropological statements that are erroneously, and more or less accidentally, derived by reification from his similar-sounding theoretical postulates. If only for the sake of making his efforts logically unassailable, the sociologist has to make it clear whether he subscribes to an image of man corresponding closely to the reified *homo sociologicus,* or whether he regards it as a caricature of man in his moral (as epistemologically distinct from his scientific) existence. Thus sociology, or more precisely the individual sociologist, in fact needs at least the rudimentary image of man that comes from taking an anthropological rather than a logical view of *homo sociologicus.*

IV

Partly implicitly, partly explicitly, the preceding argument also underlies the concluding parts of my essay "Homo Sociologicus."

This essay has happily found many thorough and incisive critics in the profession, most of whom have attacked the particular anthropological position that I take in response to the demand discussed here. This is especially true of Tenbruck's critique, which is largely based on the completely erroneous suspicion that I myself reify *homo sociologicus*: "There is thus in Dahrendorf a crass reification of the nominal concept of role. . . . His entire essay is based on the assumption that his definition of role is a definition of something real." (62: 29.)[13] As for Bahrdt, he is preaching to the converted when he argues, in criticizing my essay, "It would seem that [sociology's] long-standing semi-dependence on the mother discipline of philosophy cannot be ended so quickly. Even the methodological pluralism that prevents the inner consolidation of sociology will be with us for a long time." (46: 16.)

One important objection to the demand that the sociologist take a stand on his construct *homo sociologicus*—i.e., to make this quite clear, not the ~oncept of role but the postulate of role-conforming behavior—has been made by Arnold Gehlen (51: 368ff.). Gehlen rightly sees this demand as calling for a "political" statement (as he calls it). Invoking Max Weber, Gehlen rejects any such statement as "unscientific," especially if it is to have a " 'propagandist' effect, that is encouraging, affirming, promoting, etc.," for "at that moment it becomes agitation masquerading as science, even if it is for a worthy purpose. It is necessary that the scientist live in a given society, that he approve of its orders and political principles [*sic!*], but that he not actively support these principles." This is why the sociologist cannot legitimately be invited to try to protect himself from the possible reification of *homo sociologicus* by taking a value position, especially since "at the level of reflection reached today," a "wholesome political decision in matters of freedom" remains possible despite the extent to which scientific theories make human behavior appear determined. Schelsky probably means

---

[13] Fruitful as Tenbruck's criticism is in many details, it is based, strictly speaking, on two fundamental misunderstandings: first, that "Homo Sociologicus" is an attempt to secure the "acceptance of role theory"; second, that I subscribe to a methodological realism. These avoidable misunderstandings make an extensive rebuttal difficult.

much the same thing in his criticism of "Homo Sociologicus" for
its attitude toward the image of man and the reified *homo sociologicus*; he ends with the statement, "Moralizing has at all times been
the greatest enemy of theory, especially in sociology." (61: 108.)

Here we are faced with basic differences in scientific attitude,
differences (with one apparent exception) that cannot be resolved
unambiguously. Only the reference to the "level of reflection
reached today" (Schelsky's "scientificated world"), as an argument
that science is harmless even if it is liable to be misunderstood,
seems capable of being tested. Even here, however, closer consideration reveals that Gehlen is relatively indifferent to the measur-
able degree of people's understanding of the substance and methods
of scientific research; his concern is with more abstract secular
structures. Thus it is still an open question whether the sociologist
regards the "wholesome political decision in matters of freedom"
as a private affair, and thus lets things take their course even if
they follow from misinterpretations of his own theories; or whether
he is one of those anachronistic "happy few" who "can think and
act 'in one cast' " (whatever this means) and who, according to
Gehlen, are unqualified to be scholars.[14] Faced with the terrible
picture of a world of hypostatized *homines sociologici,* I prefer the
anachronism of enlightened moralizing, even if the authority of
Max Weber seems to justify the detachment of Gehlen and Schelsky. There is perhaps little point in quarreling over such dogmatic
statements; it would be equally possible to claim that moralizing
has at all times been the stimulus that advanced theory, especially
in sociology.

V

Obviously the objections of Gehlen and Schelsky go beyond my
belief that sociologists should decide what they think about the

---

[14] According to Gehlen, "In the twentieth century, the happy few who can think
and act 'in one cast' are best suited to be politicians and not scholars." And again,
"This is not a scientific question; *homo sociologicus* ... is a camouflaged *homo politicus orientalis.*"

probable distortions of their logically unassailable constructs, to attack the particular point of view that I proposed in "Homo Sociologicus." Since this proposal has met with intense resistance elsewhere as well, it may be worthwhile to recapitulate it briefly here.

Unfortunately a society populated by *homines sociologici*, i.e., the massive reification of the basic assumptions of sociological theories, is only too easily conceivable today. America's "lonely crowd" comes as close to being such a society as Russia's "democracy without liberty." It is by no means difficult to argue that misunderstood sociological theory serves not only as an instrument of Soviet terror, but as the ideology of American suburbia. As a science, sociology is still in its infancy; but already—contrary to the wishes, although often not the practice, of sociologists—it has developed capacities for curtailing freedom that as recently as half a century ago were conceived of only in utopian fantasy. In view of such dangers it seems to me necessary not only that the sociologist speak out in the matter of reification, but that he clearly dissociate his image of man from *homo sociologicus*. The sociologist should make it clear that for him human nature is not accurately described by the principle of role conformity, that indeed the difference between this theoretically fruitful construct and his idea of human nature amounts almost to a contradiction.

This image of man, which is so far merely privative, may be filled in in several ways. Here, I should think, is the place to return critically to the greatest thinker of the real, i.e. pre-Hegelian, enlightenment.[15] In any case, what sociological theory does not tell us about man is his moral quality; it does not show us man as we recognize him in the world of action. This moral quality of man detaches him in principle from all claims of society; it is what enables him to throw off the hypostatized regularities of sociological theory. Scientifically it may be plausible and useful to interpret the educational process as the socialization of the individual, but morally it is crucial that the individual be capable of holding his own against

---

15 Certain prejudices of intellectual history ("One cannot understand Kant without Hegel") make such a step difficult in Germany; for this reason Germans would do well to remember the broader Western tradition of the Enlightenment.

the claims of society. If the assumption of role conformity has proved extraordinarily fruitful in scientific terms, in moral terms the assumption of a permanent protest against the demands of society is much more fruitful. This is why an image of man may be developed that stresses man's inexhaustible capacity for over-coming all the forces for alienation that are inherent in the con-ception and reality of society. It need scarcely be added that this, too, would be the outline rather than the substance of an image of man; in this formulation, too, the privative element is dominant. But such a sketchy image seems good enough if one is primarily interested in sociological analysis. Although the sociologist must not evade the obligation to say what he thinks about the reified versions of his constructs, he need go no further than is strictly necessary to dissociate himself from misinterpretations of his views.[16]

Critics of this argument for a privative view of the nature of man object most of all to its direct identification of role playing with constraint. Thus Bahrdt argues plausibly, in terms of both the theory and its reified misinterpretation, that people are often free to put their individual stamp on their roles.[17] This is certainly true: "Freedom in the sense of absence of constraint does not stand in contradiction to the fact of social role playing. The very peculiarity of defining roles by expectations is that expectations only very rarely assume the character of constraint." (55: 468.) Not only do roles always leave their incumbents a range of individual choice, but also there is the phenomenon of successful deviance from ex-pectations, a phenomenon that Merton describes as "rebellion" (in contrast to "retreatism") because it leads to changes in social structure. But it is probably no accident that Bahrdt develops this argument to support his thesis that man is not a "fully adaptable

16 This is a formal objection to Judith Janoska-Bendl's argument that the notions of "individual" and "freedom" in my "Homo Sociologicus" suffer from "indefinite-ness" (55: 467, 470). Substantively, of course, there can be little doubt about the im-portance of rendering these concepts more precise; Mrs. Janoska-Bendl has made a beginning here.

17 Elsewhere (46: *passim*) Bahrdt refers time and again to the individual's "per-sonal achievement in translating role expectations into concrete terms."

creature": this, too, is a privative view of man in terms of socio-logical analysis, and thus complies with the logical and moral re-quirements set forth here.

We are taken one step further by Tenbruck and Armand Cuvil-lier, who maintain that speaking of man apart from his social per-sonality is either misleading or nonsensical. Cuvillier sees in such formulations a confusion of "individuality" and "personality," and refers to Durkheim's thesis that the personality can be realized only in society (49: 664–65). Tenbruck, somewhat rashly, goes even further: "Sociology and social psychology have shown, indepen-dently of each other, that man without roles does not and cannot exist." (62: 31.) This (though I deplore the echo of *tu quoque*) is reification,[18] or sociologism—that is, the uncritically realistic inter-pretation of scientific assumptions! The fact that in sociology and social psychology the idea of role helps explain human behavior implies absolutely nothing about the real existence of men with or without roles; it is therefore in principle irrelevant to the premises and conclusions of a philosophical theory of man. (Conversely, if such a theory refers to sociological, social psychological, or anthro-pological research in order to establish itself as "scientific," it is guilty of either a deliberate or an ignorant effort to deceive.) The statement that the human personality can realize itself only in so-ciety does not follow from role analysis, and does not make it any the less necessary to hold up against a hypostatized *homo sociologi-cus* a moral image of the human person.

There remains, however, one serious objection to consider, a point first raised by Plessner, adopted by Tenbruck at one point in his critique, and at least implied by Judith Janoska-Bendl. This objection is apposite because it makes its appeal to precisely the level of pragmatic logic that I have invoked earlier in this essay. Plessner argues that by contrasting the moral personality of man with the significance of society for the individual, we not only revive the unhappy distinction between a public and a private

---

[18] There is some danger that sociologists today will keep on charging one another with "reification" just as the thinkers of the Hegelian Left once kept on accusing each other of being "theologians."

existence, but actually imply a preference for the private existence, and thus lend support to the "unpolitical German":

> If sociology finds itself prepared in principle to separate being in a role from the real being of the self, and to uphold the real being against the vexation of society (as Dahrendorf has recently done with his *homo sociologicus*), then it gives new support to the antisocial affect, whether it intends to or not. If in order to make the sphere of freedom unassailable we identify it with that of privacy (and privacy, we should note, in an extra-social sense), freedom loses all contact with reality, all possibility of social realization. (59: 114–15.)

More emphatically still, and with reference to another of Plessner's writings, Tenbruck refers to the German "tradition that distinguishes society from the individual and sees the social being as alienated—a tradition to which the history of literature, of philosophy, of politics, bears telling testimony. On this point, social traditions and the intellectual approach to social questions lead to the same misunderstanding: sociological concepts are turned upside down." (62: 37.) Very reservedly and yet with unmistakable intent, Janoska-Bendl asks "why, with respect to the role-playing (because socialized) man, the Hegelian—or Marxian—dialectical solution is not even considered." Earlier, she mentions Plessner's and Tenbruck's point that the individual, "as a mature social ego, is capable of reshaping his role, determining himself what it shall be, and thus—dialectically—going beyond it" (55: 473, 469).

These objections are too serious and too important to be dismissed with a few quick remarks. It is quite true that few things illustrate the lack of a bourgeois revolution in German history more clearly than the unpolitical German. But it is important here to distinguish clearly between two attitudes which only superficially resemble each other: that of the "inner emigrant," and that of the liberal. Plessner and Tenbruck claim that in a theory of man in which society functions as a vexation, the individual must necessarily be seen as turning away from social and political affairs and thus as becoming irresponsible; such a theory is analogous to Heidegger's "theory of human decadence in the deficient mood of the 'one,' " which as Plessner rightly remarks "is spoken right out of the soul of German 'inwardness' " (59: 140). But both Plessner and Tenbruck forget that there is another confrontation of the two—society and the individual—in which the motive of protest is dominant. The individual as a moral being, as a living protest against the vexation of society; Riesman's "inner-directed man"; the political resistance to society's claim to dictate man's every move—these are the liberal conceptions that have led me to make the statements to which Plessner and Tenbruck object. Perhaps such statements are especially likely to be misunderstood in Germany; for in fact I was aiming at something quite different from the "transcendental reflection" that Schelsky believes in and at times imputes to me, and on which Janoska-Bendl considers my views and hers identical.[19] The possibility of this misunderstanding seems to justify Plessner's objections. But that an unresigned political protest against the alienating forces of society is possible seems to me one of the great lessons of the Anglo-Saxon liberal tradition.

Janoska-Bendl is right in her assumption that a view of this kind involves an irreconcilable antinomy (to associate in her sense Kant and Kierkegaard). The search for conciliation, from which German moral philosophy has been suffering ever since Fichte, does not seem to me a path to liberty even under the colorful name of dialectics. Janoska-Bendl cautiously suggests that "freedom as insight into necessity" also permits "using force to accomplish liberty" (55: 486). There is a strange dialectic of dialectics in the fact that this "also" is the regular consequence of the attempt to apply dialectics to reality. Why do so many find it so hard to discover freedom in the antinomic existence of man?

Bahrdt concludes his essay on images of man in sociology with the somewhat disappointed observation that there probably is no compelling image of this kind after all. In substance I should agree with him, but without sharing his disappointment. With respect to our knowledge of human nature, sociology is in a difficult and contradictory position. Its theories basically have nothing to do

---

19 Cf. Schelsky (61: 108): "Dahrendorf comes ... closest to the kind of transcendental theory of sociology we have sketched."

with the essence of man. But since these theories are based on assumptions that may be misinterpreted by those who do not know
or accept the conventions of scientific research, sociology is obliged
to pronounce on such misinterpretations. In the nature of the case,
any such pronouncement is compelling only in its logical substance.
Beyond that there is no sociological view of human nature, as there
is no generally compelling image of man, but only more or less con-
vincing attacks on the problem. Perhaps philosophy is always definable as thought with a moral intention. In any event, differences
in the philosophic realm cannot harm the development of sociology. Images of man, too, belong in that sphere of para-theory where
the most fruitful stimuli for new theories may originate, even if
the stimuli themselves are personal rather than testable by experience.

References

References

The following references are grouped alphabetically by chapter; titles are numbered consecutively throughout the volume, however, to facilitate citation in the text.

1. *Homo Sociologicus*

This essay was written in 1957, at the Center for Advanced Study in the Behavioral Sciences, Stanford, California, under the influence of discussions with a number of friends, among whom I should like to mention Joseph Ben-David (Jerusalem), Philip Rieff (Philadelphia), and Fritz Stern (New York), as well as Hellmut Geissner, then my colleague as Saarbrücken. This essay was part of a *Festschrift* presented to my philosophy teacher Josef König on the occasion of his sixty-fifth birthday, February 24, 1958. It was first published, in two installments, in the *Kölner Zeitschrift für Soziologie* (Vol. X, Nos. 2–3) in 1958. A year later Westdeutsche Verlag published a separate edition, which has since gone through five printings. (An Italian edition of the essay appeared in 1966.) The essay appeared in *Essays in the Theory of Society* with permission of the publisher.

The Preface gives some indication of the lively debate provoked by this essay. Some of the contributions to that debate are listed below, in the references to this essay and to its postscript, "Sociology and Human Nature." To do justice to the large number of publications on the subject of roles that have appeared since "Homo Sociologicus" was written would require a thorough revision; if I have not undertaken this task here, it it because I see the main point of the essay as critical and philosophical rather than strictly sociological. By way of a further exploration of its sociological aspects, I hope soon to publish a short treatise *On Social Roles*.

1. M. Banton. Roles: An Introduction to the Study of Social Relations. London: Tavistock, 1965.
2. B. Barber. Social Stratification. New York: Harcourt, Brace, 1965.
3. C. I. Barnard. "The Functions and Pathology of Status Systems in Formal Organizations." In Industry and Society, ed. W. F. Whyte. New York: McGraw-Hill, 1946.
4. J. Ben-David. "Professionals and Unions in Israel." Industrial Relations, Vol. V, No. 1 (1965).
5. J. W. Bennett and M. M. Tumin. Social Life: Structure and Function. New York: Alfred A. Knopf, 1952.
6. Cicero. De officiis.
7. E. R. Curtius. Europäische Literatur und Lateinisches Mittelalter. Bern: Huber, 1948.
8. R. Dahrendorf. Class and Class Conflict in Industrial Society. Stanford, Calif.: Stanford University Press (1959), ⁴1965. British edition, London: Routledge & Kegan Paul, ³1963.
9. K. Davis. Human Society. New York: Macmillan, 1949.
10. E. Durkheim. Règles de la méthode sociologique. Paris: Presses Universitaires de France, 1950.
11. S. N. Eisenstadt. From Generation to Generation: Age Groups and Social Structure. Chicago, Ill.: Free Press, 1956.
12. H. H. Gerth and C. W. Mills. Character and Social Structure. New York: Harcourt, Brace, 1964. British edition, London: Routledge & Kegan Paul, 1954.
13. N. Gross, W. S. Mason, and A. W. McEachern. Explorations in Role Analysis. New York: John Wiley, 1958.
14. P. R. Hofstätter. Sozialpsychologie. Berlin: De Gruyter, 1956.
15. ———. Gruppendynamik. Reinbek: Rowohlt, 1957.
16. G. Homans. The Human Group. London: Routledge & Kegan Paul, 1951.
17. A. Inkeles and D. J. Levinson. "National Character: The Study of Modal Personality and Sociocultural Systems." In Handbook of Social Psychology, ed. G. Lindzey. Cambridge, Mass.: Addison-Wesley, 1954.
18. I. Kant. Kritik der reinen Vernunft. Ed. R. Schmidt. Leipzig: Meiner, ²1932.
19. R. Linton. The Study of Man. New York: Appleton-Century, 1936.
20. ———. "Role and Status." In Readings in Social Psychology, ed. T. H. Newcomb and E. L. Hartley. New York: Henry Holt, 1957.
21. T. H. Marshall. "A Note on Status." In Professor Ghurye Felicitation Volume, ed. K. M. Kapadia. Bombay, 1954.
22. K. Marx. Das Kapital. New ed. Berlin: Dietz, 1953.
23. M. Mead. Male and Female: A Study of the Sexes in a Changing World. New York: Morrow, 1949.
24. R. K. Merton. Social Theory and Social Structure. Rev. ed. Chicago, Ill.: Free Press, 1957.
25. H. A. Murray. "Toward a Classification of Interaction." In 54.
26. R. Musil. Der Mann ohne Eigenschaften. Reinbek: Rowohlt, 1952.

27. S. F. Nadel. The Foundations of Social Anthropology. London: Cohen & West, 1950.
28. ——. The Theory of Social Structure. London: Cohen & West (1957), ²1962.
29. L. J. Neiman and J. W. Hughes. "The Problem of the Concept of Role: A Re-Survey of the Literature." Social Forces, Vol. XXX (1951).
30. T. Parsons. The Structure of Social Action. New York: McGraw-Hill, 1937.
31. ——. The Social System. Chicago, Ill.: Free Press, 1951. British edition, London: Routledge & Kegan Paul, 1952.
32. ——, and E. A. Shils, eds. Toward a General Theory of Action. Cambridge, Mass.: Harvard University Press, 1951.
33. Plato. Laws.
34. Plato. Philebus.
35. H. Popitz. Der Begriff der sozialen Rolle als Element der soziologischen Theorie. Tübingen: Mohr (Siebeck), 1967.
36. A. R. Radcliffe-Brown. Structure and Function in Primitive Society. London: Cohen & West, 1952.
37. B. Russell. Human Knowledge: Its Scope and Limits. London: Allen & Unwin, 1948.
38. T. R. Sarbin. "Role Theory." In Handbook of Social Psychology, ed. G. Lindzey. Cambridge, Mass.: Addison-Wesley, 1954.
39. K. F. Schumann. "Zur Theorie und Praxis der Messung sozialer Sanktionen." Tübingen: philosophy dissertation, 1967.
40. Seneca. Epistolae morales.
41. N. J. Smelser. Social Change in the Industrial Revolution. Chicago: University of Chicago Press, 1959. British edition, London: Routledge & Kegan Paul, 1959.
42. F. Stern, ed. The Varieties of History. New York: Doubleday, ²1957.
43. A. Weber. Einführung in die Soziologie. München: Piper, 1955.
44. M. Weber. Gesammelte Aufsätze zur Wissenschaftslehre. Tübingen: Mohr (Siebeck) (1923), ²1951.

2. Sociology and Human Nature

In 1962, when Andreas Flitner, then my colleague at Tübingen, invited me to contribute to a volume he was editing on philosophical anthropology—Wege zur pädagogischen Anthropologie (Heidelberg: Quelle & Meyer [1963], ²1967)—I took the opportunity to answer some of the critics of "Homo Sociologicus." In the fourth printing of that essay, the reply appeared as an appendix. Its shortcomings are obvious: after a brief summary of role analysis, it proceeds rapidly to a somewhat esoteric debate; it does not answer all the charges initially made against "Homo Sociologicus"; and it does not, of course, deal at all with critical studies published after it was written (some of which are listed below).

It seems to me, however, that the main methodological point of this brief rejoinder remains valid.

45. Aristotle. Politics.
46. H. P. Bahrdt. "Zur Frage des Menschenbildes in der Soziologie." *European Journal of Sociology*, Vol. II (1961).
47. R. F. Beerling. "Homo Sociologicus: Een kritiek op Dahrendorf." *Mens en Maatschappij*, Vol. XXXVIII (1963).
48. D. Claessens. "Rolle und Verantwortung." *Soziale Welt*, Vol. XIV, No. 1 (1963).
49. A. Cuvillier. Review of "Homo Sociologicus." *Kyklos*, Vol. XII, No. 4 (1959).
50. E. Garczyk. "Der Homo Sociologicus und der Mensch in der Gesellschaft." *In* Mensch, Gesellschaft, Geschichte: F. D. E. Schleiermachers philosophische Soziologie. München: Uni-Druck, 1963.
51. A. Gehlen. Review of "Homo Sociologicus." *Zeitschrift für die gesamte Staatswissenschaft*, Vol. CXVII, No. 2 (1961).
52. H. Geissner. "Soziale Rollen als Sprechrollen." *Allgemeine und angewandte Phonetik* (1960).
53. J. Habermas. Theorie und Praxis: Sozialphilosophische Studien. Neuwied-Berlin: Luchterhand, 1963.
54. ———. "Zur Logik der Sozialwissenschaften," Philosophische Rundschau (Beiheft 5). Tübingen: Mohr (Siebeck), 1967.
55. J. Janoska-Bendl. "Probleme der Freiheit in der Rollenanalyse." *Kölner Zeitschrift für Soziologie*, Vol. XIV, No. 3 (1962).
56. R. König, ed. Soziologie (Fischer-Lexikon 10). Frankfurt: Fischer, 1958.
57. ———. "Freiheit und Selbstentfremdung in soziologischer Sicht." *In* Freiheit als Problem der Wissenschaft. Berlin: De Gruyter, 1962.
58. L. Phillipps. Zur Ontologie der sozialen Rolle. Frankfurt: Klostermann, 1963.
59. H. Plessner. "Soziale Rollen und menschliche Natur." *In* Erkenntnis und Verantwortung: Festschrift für Th. Litt. Düsseldorf: Diederichs, 1960.
60. ———. "Ungesellige Geselligkeit." *In* Die moderne Demokratie und ihr Recht: Festschrift für Gerhard Leibholz. Tübingen: Mohr (Siebeck), 1966.
61. H. Schelsky. Ortsbestimmung der deutschen Soziologie. Düsseldorf-Köln: Diederichs, 1959.
62. F. H. Tenbruck. "Zur deutschen Rezeption der Rollentheorie." *Kölner Zeitschrift für Soziologie*, Vol. XIII, No. 1 (1961).

Index

Index

For Product Safety Concerns and Information please contact our EU
representative GPSR@taylorandfrancis.com
Taylor & Francis Verlag GmbH, Kaufingerstraße 24, 80331 München, Germany